HERE'S WHAT ABOUT

MW00522916

- "The *Pennsylvania Gun La* nian who has a gun or is thinking about getting one."
  Mike Slavonic, *NRA Board of Directors* Chairman,
  Allegheny County Sportsmen's Leag

- "Common sense *isn't enough* to avoid the traps in Pennsylvania's new gun laws. Ken Abel's book is an *indispensable* guide."
  Harry Schneider, Chairman, Legislative Committee,
  Pennsylvania Sportsmen's Association

- What hurts you is *not* what you *don't know* it's what you *think* you know, that's *wrong!* Even if you've owned guns for 30 years, *I guarantee* this book will tell you things that you thought you knew, but which are *wrong!* And that can save you from losing your guns . . . or your freedom.
  Dennis Pavlik, Vice-Chairman, *Pennsylvania Sportsmen's*
  Association; Vice-Pres., Firearms Owners Against Crime

- "Pennsylvania gun owners are lucky to have Ken's excellent firearms law resource!"
  Attorney John Machtinger, author of
  "How to Own a Gun & Stay Out of Jail - California"

- "Pennsylvania's new gun laws are filled with legalistic land mines that gun owners can step on. This book tells us where to watch our step."
  Andy Barniskis, Legislative Chairman,
  Bucks County Sportsmen's Coalition

- "When it comes to guns, 'ignorance of the law' can cost you money or even land you in jail. Knowing what's in this book, can help ensure that neither of these things happens to you."
  Attorney J. Michael McCormick, participating member,
  NRA Attorney Referral Service

- "The *Pennsylvania Gun Law Guide* should sit on the desk of every Law Enforcement Official . ... and on the bookshelf of anyone who owns a gun. Many people who own guns are clueless about how much trouble they can actually get into from a simple indiscretion . . . By using Mr. Abel's book as a guide you provide for . . . your *legal survival.*
  Bob Swartzwelder, Senior SWAT Trainer, Police Trainer, Police
  Officer, Western Pennsylvania

DON'T MISS...

. . .THIS IMPORTANT INFORMATION FOUND AT THE <u>BACK</u> OF THIS BOOK

Pennsylvania GUN LAW Update

The book you are reading will tell you everything that's known about how the new gun laws affect current, and would-be, gun owners, as of October 1996. But changes in these laws - to eliminate "traps" that could take away your guns . . . or your freedom - are being proposed by gun owners organizations. We will publish all the upcoming changes in the *GUN LAW Update*. Information on how to obtain the *Update* is at the back of this book.

Learn how to get a copy of the *Pennsylvania Sportsmen's News* - with information on who, in our state and federal government is on the side of gun owners, and who is not. You *can't always tell* by what the legislators say . . . because many of them tell two completely different stories! Get the truth from the *Pennsylvania Sportsmen's News*.

SPORTSMEN'S CLUBS, RETAILERS & BOOKSTORES SELL THIS BOOK!

Are you a *retailer* that wants to sell this book to your customers? Or a *gun club* that wants to offer this book to members to help raise money? What you need to know can be found at the back of this book.

GUN OWNERS: NEED ANOTHER COPY OF THIS BOOK

Want *more copies* of this book but *can't find* a source? There's a handy order form at the back of this book that you can use to order more copies direct from the publisher.

Ken Abel's

P E N N S Y L V A N I A
GUN LAW GUIDE

What Every Handgun, Rifle, or Shotgun Owner
MUST KNOW* About Pennsylvania and Federal Gun Laws

Or else, all your guns could be **confiscated,
you could be forced to **pay big fines**,
or you could be **sent to jail**.*

Kenneth F. Abel

Published by
ABELexpress
230 East Main Street
Carnegie, Pennsylvania 15106
412-279-0672

96   97   98   99   10   9   8   7   6   5   4   3   2   1

ISBN 0-944214-07-X

ACKNOWLEDGEMENTS

Behind the pages of every book is an author: and behind every author is usually a core group of people who helped turn the author's ideas into a coherent, finished product. This book is no exception; and the author would like to express his gratitude to the people who helped make this book a reality.

Harry Schneider, Legislative Chairman of the *Pennsylvania Sportsmen's Association*, knows more about the history of guns and gun laws than you'll find in one book . . . or a hundred books. He gave unselfishly of his time to guide me through the intricate web of laws, regulations and court decisions that govern gun ownership. Harry proved that despite the most noble legislative intent, poorly conceived gun control laws put respectable gun owners in jeopardy while making it easier for criminals to prey upon honest citizens. He also pointed out how bad gun control laws can, unfortunately, drive a wedge between the police and good citizens. A very highly trained practical shooter, Harry volunteers to help train and assist police just as he volunteers to help the Pennsylvania Legislature avoid legislation that is destructive to freedom. Harry says that he likes the police but despises a police state, just as he hates real criminals and doesn't want the legislature to make criminals of honest citizens. His enormous network of friends and contacts all use the same word to describe him: "effective."

J. Michael McCormick, Attorney at Law, of Verona, Pa., a member of the *Pennsylvania Sportsmen's Association*, has an extensive understanding of Pennsylvania's firearms laws, and strongly supports the fundamental right of Americans to keep and bear arms. Mike was kind enough to review the manuscript and provide valuable assistance.

Mike Slavonic and **Kim Stolfer**, Chairman and Vice-Chairman, respectively, of the *Allegheny County Sportsmen's League*, and **Andy Barniskis**, of the *Bucks County Sportsmen's Coalition*, also made their expertise available to me.

Dennis Pavlik, Political Affairs Coordinator of the *Crowfoot Rod and Gun Club,* Vice-Chairman of the *Pennsylvania Sportsmen's Association,* and Vice-President of *Firearms Owners Against Crime,* brought to my attention several matters which are of great importance to gun owners.

Also on the legal side, attorney **John Machtinger**, of Los Angeles, Ca., and author of *How to Own a Gun & Stay Out of Jail - California*, made many valuable suggestions that helped make this book more readable and more informative.

On the home front, **Sandy Swenglish**, our staff graphic artist, re-typeset this book about four zillion times, as changes were made, again and again, to enhance readability and comprehension, and to take into account the continuing changes in the gun laws and their likely interpretation by law enforcement agencies and the judiciary. Sandy is also responsible for the design of the cover.

And finally, I would like to extend thanks to my family - my wife, Jackie, and our four kids, Jeremy, Joshua, Jessica and Joanna - who put up with my frequent absences as we worked on the book day and night.

To anyone whose name I should have mentioned but didn't, I extend my apologies - and sincerest thanks.

K.F.A.

DISCLAIMER - READ THIS FIRST

This book is a summary of selected, important laws, primarily about *guns*. Laws which deal specifically with weapons other than guns (for example, explosives) are excluded from this book, unless they happen to be part of an included law relating to guns. Neither this book, nor any book, can include all the laws that might apply to any situation. Your belief that information in this book would apply to your situation might not be correct. *Do not take any action, or decide not to take any action, until you read and understand each part of this disclaimer.*

☐ *This book provides general, informational material only.* It does not give legal advice. Do not rely on this book to predict how the law will be applied to you. Do not use this book as a substitute for an attorney.

☐ *The legislature passes laws about guns; the courts interpret those laws.* The courts' interpretations of the laws may be entirely different from what anyone might conclude from simply reading the laws or our comments about the laws, as they are printed in this book. You could, for example, read this book and decide that an action is completely *lawful*; only to discover that the courts have interpreted or expanded the law so that the action, is actually *unlawful*. Only an attorney can advise you as to whether a particular action is, or is not, lawful.

☐ *This book includes only Pennsylvania and federal laws.* Do not use this book as a guide to the laws of other states. It is important that you understand that certain federal laws are known to have superseded *(taken the place of)* certain Pennsylvania laws. For example, Pennsylvania law requires a *48 hour* waiting period before taking possession of a handgun that you have purchased; federal law, with its *5 day* waiting period supersedes Pennsylvania law.

☐ ***Laws change.*** New laws, or changes to existing laws may have been enacted that supersede, change or expand the laws that are printed in this book . . . so what is completely ***lawful today*** could be ***unlawful tomorrow!*** It is your responsibility to keep up with changes and additions made to the law.

☐ Even though ***headings***, such as "Game and Wildlife," and "Sale of Firearms," are used throughout this book, the use of the headings is not meant to imply that all laws on that subject are included.

☐ ***Special exceptions*** to some laws (and to our comments about some laws) usually exist for law enforcement officers and members of the armed forces on active duty and for certain others. Exceptions of the "opposite" type usually exist for persons who ***intend*** to commit a crime. Many of these exceptions are not mentioned in this book.

☐ The author and publisher of this book, and those he consulted while drafting it, are not responsible for any legal or economic result of any outcome of any situation involving guns or other devices mentioned in this book; and they are not responsible for errors or omissions in the reporting of the law, or in their comments; and they are not responsible for changes or additions to the law that are not reported in this book.

Remember, the purpose of this book is to provide informational material, not to give legal advice. All the laws that apply to your situation may not be printed in this book. The courts, the Pennsylvania legislature or the the federal government may have changed or added to the laws, or the interpretation of the laws, or our explanations that are printed in this book. Consult an attorney before you take any action, or decide not to take any action, as a result of reading this book.

CONTENTS

INTRODUCTION

Do you own a rifle, shotgun or handgun?

Or, are you considering the purchase of a gun for your own use, or for your spouse or a child or grandchild?

If your answer to either question is "yes," then it is important to remember that gun ownership brings with it the responsiblility of *understanding the laws* that govern the gun's possession and use. A hundred years ago, about the only gun laws on the books concerned the use of guns in major crimes such as murder. But today there are thousands of laws - federal, state and local - that regulate the "possession, use, manufacture, control, sale and transfer of firearms."

The words in quotes, above, were quite a mouthful, weren't they. But those were not our words. Those words were taken directly from the new Pennsylvania gun law, Act 17 of the Special Session on Crime (hereafter referred to as "Act 17"), which was enacted on June 13, 1995, and which went into effect October 11, 1995. All those words you just read were in the "title" of one small section of the law. And if that's the title of just one little section, you can imagine how complex and hard to understand, the rest of the new law - all 10-15,000 words of it - must be.

So, recognizing that "ignorance of the law is no excuse" (no matter how complex, confusing and contradictory the laws may be), what can you do to help ensure that you are in compliance with those laws? Well, one thing you can do is to read this book. The whole purpose of this book is to translate the most important of those gun-related statutes (laws) from "legalese" into ordinary English that anyone can read and understand.

To make the statutes even easier to understand, we've turned all the information into a series of simple questions and answers. We *ask* the questions that *you* would be most likely to ask . . . and

1

then we **answer** those questions in a simple and forthright manner. These Questions and Answers are what you'll find in Part I of this book.

What if you want more information than is in our answer? Well, that's no problem, because in Part II of this book, we print the entire text of the applicable Pennsylvania statute (insofar as it relates to guns), so that you can read the law exactly the way your legislators wrote it.

We've also included a statute index - so if you know of a Pennsylvania statute (law) that applies in your situation, you can check the statute index and find the page in this book on which it is printed.

Here's a couple of examples to show you how easy it is to use this book.

1. **You have a question.** Example: *At what age can my kid own or use an air rifle?*

2. **Go to the Part I Table of Contents.** Read the list until you find a matching question. Example: You find *"Minimum ages for hunting, gun ownership and use," which is on page 31.*

3. **Turn to the listed page.** Read the complete question . . . and the answer.

4. **Want more info?** You can read the statute exactly as it's written. Example: *Underneath the answer is the citation of the applicable statute,* 18 Pa. C.S. § 6304. *Go to the statute index, Part III, which lists Pennsylvania statutes in numerical sequence, and find that the statute is on page 112 of this book.*

5. **Turn to that page and read the entire statute.**

Now, suppose *you* have a question but can't find a match with one of *our* questions. Or suppose you have a *very general* question or want to read all the statutes in a particular category, such as "Game and Wildlife"?. Here's what you do.

1. **You want to see all - or most - of the laws that apply in a particular situation.** Example: *You were a bit wild when you were younger, and you don't know if your misbehavior was sufficient to prevent you from owning a gun. You would like to see exactly what the laws say about that.*

2. **Go to the Part II Table of Contents.** Read down and find a likely match. Example: *You find "Persons Not to Possess, Use, Manufacture, Control, Sell or Transfer Guns," which is on page 82.*

3. **Turn to that page and read the statute exactly as it's written.**

Isn't that pretty simple?

Now, before you jump into this book to find the answers to all those questions you've been collecting for years, but for which no one had an answer, please read the important information that follows.

We've already told you about Pennsylvania's new gun law, Act 17, which took effect on October 11, 1995. Unfortunately, legislative action on Act 17 was taken very hurriedly, before knowledgeable gun owners could make suggestions. As a result there were significant problems with many parts of the Act.

For example, Act 17 made it illegal for minors (persons under 18 years of age) to possess or use a rifle or shotgun without adult supervision. Thus, youths aged 16-18 could no longer hunt by themselves, a privilege they had previously enjoyed for many, many years.

Needless to say, once "the word" about Act 17 got out to hunters and other gun owners, screams of disapproval could be heard all the way to Harrisburg. To fix the many problems with Act 17 people knowledgeable about gun laws suggested a number of amendments. The Pennsylvania legislature included some of these amendments in Senate Bill 282, which became Act 66 when it was signed by Governor Ridge on November 22, 1995.

Act 66 was beneficial in that it changed some of the more onerous parts of Act 17 - such as the elimination of the right of 16-18 year olds to hunt without adult supervision. But Act 66 did not address many other major issues, such as the apparent loss of the right to buy rifles and shotguns in other states.

As you can see, Acts 17 and 66 affect *every* owner of a handgun, rifle or shotgun. To keep informed as to what you are allowed to do with your guns - and what you are *not* allowed to do - we offer an update - a complete listing and commentary on all the changes made to Pennsylvania gun laws, including Acts 17 and 66, as they continue to be enacted, after the publication date of this book. *(See the form at the back of this book for details of this offer.)*

And finally . . . when this book was written we had the choice of providing general answers to general questions . . . or turning the book into a technical manual, replete with footnotes and case law. We elected to keep the book simple and comprehensible, with the understanding that what you read may not be the "final answer" to your question . . . but it will be a darn good starting point.

Thanks for picking up our book. We hope you enjoy reading it as much as we enjoyed writing it. And we hope that the information you get from this book will help you enjoy and use your guns in a safe and legal manner.

ACT 17

Act 17 is the set of new statutes (laws) pertaining to guns (handguns, rifles and shotguns) that was enacted by the Pennsylvania legislature on June 13, 1995 and which took effect October 11, 1995.

The purpose of Act 17 was to reduce crime. However, Act 17 (known as House Bill 110 in its original form, before it was signed into law) was written and passed very hurriedly, with insufficient input from gun owners and those knowledgeable about gun law. *As a result, Act 17 contains many provisions which could be harmful to Pennsylvania gun owners.* By "harmful" we don't mean just "inconvenient." In the words of J. Michael McCormick, J.D., a Verona, Pennsylvania attorney:

> *". . . I became very concerned about the dangers [Act 17] creates for the typical, honest, law-abiding gun owner of Pennsylvania, or possible future gun owner, who might also enjoy hunting, dog training, fishing or target shooting.*
>
> *The 'law-abiding' status of many Pennsylvanians will be placed in jeopardy as a result of the difficulty in comprehending and complying with [Act 17's] many provisions. In the future, an honest, otherwise law-abiding Pennsylvanian might unhappily discover that he or she has unknowingly, violated some provision of this Act and is being [criminally] prosecuted for having commited a misdemeanor or even a felony offense.*
>
> ***Honest citizens, including licensed firearms dealers, who had no intention to violate any law might fall into one of the many dangerous traps found in this new firearms law and discover that they are being prosecuted for a crime they never intended to commit and didn't even know they had committed.***
>
> *Pennsylvanians have survived bad gun laws before [the enactment of] Act 17. They did so because the vast majority of police officers, prosecutors, and judges displayed more common sense than the legislature. Unfortunately, there are a few police*

5

officers, prosecutors and judges who are prejudiced against gun owners and who may use some of the poorly drafted parts of Act 17 to devastate the lives of good citizens.

Possessing, obtaining and transferring a firearm in Pennsylvania has now become potentially very dangerous to every gun owner's status as a law abiding citizen."

Here are other quotations taken from **discussions among your elected representatives** on the floor of the Pennsylvania House of Representatives, illustrating their concerns about the dangers of Act 17 (House Bill 110).

Rep. Teresa Brown: "House Bill 110 is forty four pages of gun control. . . . Gun control increases crime . . . I would ask all of you to slow this down and take a look at what this bill really does."

Rep. Scott Hutchinson: **"I also believe that the rank and file members of the sportsmen's clubs across this Commonwealth are not aware of the contents of this bill . . .** *We do not need more gun control and therefore I am opposing HB 110."*

(Emphasis by author.)

ACT 66

In response to the outcry from Pennsylvania gun owners, Pennsylvania legislators assembled a group of "technical amendments" to correct some of the ambiguities and errors of Act 17. The amendments were added to Senate Bill Number 282, which, after signing by Governor Tom Ridge, on November 22, 1995, became Act 66.

Many parts of Act 66 went into effect on the day of its signing; thus, some parts of Act 17 that were "fixed" by Act 66, were in effect for only the 45 day period that elapsed between the effective dates of Act 17 and of Act 66. We therefore make no mention of those parts of Act 17 beyond what might have already been presented in the Introduction.

Despite the changes in Act 17, however, there are still significant problems with the Act which were not addressed or corrected by Act 66. Thus, the next part of this book describes:

SPECIFIC CONCERNS ABOUT ACTS 17 & 66

Following is a list of some - *but not all* - of the concerns about Acts 17 & 66 and how these new laws affect law-abiding Pennsylvania gun owners. Although the word "firearm" is used throughout, that word has many different meanings; to avoid confusion we will use the word "gun" below, in many cases, with the understanding that we are speaking *generically* and may be referring *only* to handguns, *or* to rifles, shotguns and handguns, *collectively.*

- Portions of the Acts are *difficult to comprehend;* and it may take many years for the courts to sort out the real meaning of the law . . . or to proclaim the meaning that they want those portions to have, based on their personal feelings or prejudices.

- The Acts require that legally carried guns be checked before entering certain parts of a courthouse and that secure lockers be provided for that purpose. The Acts *do not* provide for *exceptions* if the courthouse does not offer the mandated secure and safe checking facility, a matter of great concern to those who would use public transportation to travel to the courthouse or for those uncomfortable with leaving a handgun in a car from which it can be stolen.

- The Acts *do not* mandate reasonable *limits* to the instantaneous background check fee. Thus, in five years, when the fee is next allowed to increase, it could rise to levels which would be prohibitive to the average law-abiding Pennsylvanian.

- Although the legislature expressed their intent to *eliminate the 48 hour waiting period* for a handgun purchase after the instantaneous background check was in place, the Acts are worded in such a way that the waiting period *does not* appear to have been eliminated.   And, the Acts do not exempt *any-one* from the instantaneous background check thus requiring the background check - and fee - from such persons as law enforcement officers when they purchase guns. Also *not exempt* are individuals who are designated by the district attorney as persons who need immediate access to a gun because of a threat to their life. If the computerized background check system were "down," these people, law enforcement officers, and others might not be able to obtain a gun for a minimum of 48 hours.

- If it is reported that a person is acting irrationally, and may be a danger to themselves or to others, that person can be involuntarily committed to a mental health facility for examination. The person is to be examined by a "physician"; and even if the physician concluded that "there is absolutely nothing wrong," that person will lose the right to own guns under the Acts unless that conclusion is reached within *two hours* of the time of commitment - a virtual impossibility. If more than 2 hours elapse the person is required to petition the court for expungement of the record of commitment in order to regain his/her guns. Additionally a "physician" can be a general practitioner, an ophthalmologist or even a proctologist . . . but *not* a clinical psychologist. Thus, Act 66 actually *specifies* that an *unqualified* professional may carry out the examination and *prohibits* a *qualified* professional from doing so.

Consider also, a person who became depressed after the death of a loved one, 20 years ago, and who, after saying "How can I live without him/her," was hospitalized for a few days under the authority of § 302 of the Mental Health statutes, as a precaution against suicide. Because the Acts' prohibitions against possession of guns after confinement under § 302 may be interpreted as applying retroactively, that person, now, 20 years later, could be forced to give up the guns he/she may have owned for those 20 years.

- According to Act 17, persons who were not allowed to own guns were required to divest themselves of their guns at the "instant" they were no longer allowed to own them. The word "divest" is used here because these persons were also not allowed to sell or transfer the guns; so the only alternative was to surrender them to the authorities - which was the same as confiscation. Act 66 gives such persons 60 days to get rid of their guns; but specifies that the guns cannot be sold or given to anyone in the same household. And worse, this could be interpreted to imply that all persons living in a home with a prohibited person could be burdened with a virtually-impossible-to-comply-with requirement that their own guns be made inaccessible to the prohibited person; or could even result in the loss of their own, Constitutionally protected right, to own guns.

- Act 17 may make felons out of many law abiding adults who had no criminal intent. For example, a husband, who possesses the required License which allows him to carry a concealed handgun leaves the handgun in the console of his Bronco. His wife, who does not have a License, uses the Bronco to make a quick trip to the supermarket. If she is caught with the gun in the Bronco, she is subject to arrest, prosecution and imprisonment for committing a third degree felony. Even if sentence is suspended, because she had no criminal intent, if convicted, she is prohibited from owning a gun of any kind for the rest of her life and must give up any guns she owns . . . and she cannot even give them to her husband, if they live in the same house.

- Prior to the enactment of Act 17 Pennsylvania never had a waiting period for the purchase of long guns - rifles and shotguns. But Act 17 *does* require the check; and if the instant check computer "goes down," rifles and shotguns cannot be delivered for a minimum of 48 hours.

- Acts 17 and 66 allow Pennsylvania residents to sell personally owned rifles and shotguns; but they also provide for civil liability that could lead to financially devastating lawsuits against the individuals and dealers who sold the guns.

- Federal law, as described later in the text, allows the residents of any state to purchase long guns in any other state, if the dealer in the other state has *"actual knowledge"* that the purchase does not violate the laws of *either* state. After January 1, 1997, as a result of Act 66, the instantaneous background check requirement goes into effect for long guns, in Pennsylvania. It will be a virtual impossibility for dealers in other states to access Pennsylvania's computer system; therefore they will not be able to perform a background check. Thus, they cannot comply with Pennsylvania law, which requires the background check. Without the background check selling a long gun to a Pennsylvanian would violate Pennsylvania law; and therefore, in accordance with federal law, dealers may not be permitted to sell long guns to Pennsylvanians. As a result, any hunter, target shooter or other person who travels to another state and loses his guns as the result of theft, destruction in an accident, loss by an airline or . . . , may be unable to replace those guns in that other state.

Recent (late 1996) conversations with the BATF indicate that their interpretation of the law is such that sales to Pennsylvanians by out-of-state dealers may be acceptable to them. However, analysis of the law and of its interpretation by the BATF, indicates a potential major problem for Pennsylvanians who need to purchase long guns out of state. The details of this problem, and how gun rights organizations are trying to solve it, are presented in this book, in the answer to the question concerning out-of-state purchases of long guns.

We should state again that the above are by no means all of the concerns that have been expressed about the Acts, which have the potential of turning unwitting gun owners into criminals.

FUTURE AMENDMENTS TO ACTS 17 & 66

Is there a solution to the host of problems enumerated above (and others not listed)? Yes, there is. The legislative committees of the Allegheny County Sportsmen's League (ACSL), and the Pennsylvania Sportmen's Association (PSA) have drafted "Grass Roots Reforms" which, if enacted into law by the Pennsylvania Legislature, will remove most of the known, unintended consequences of Acts 17 and 66.

For more complete information on the problems with the Acts, and on other gun issues of great importance to Pennsylvanians, please refer to recent issues of the *Pennsylvania Sportsmen's News*, published by the *Pennsylvania Sportsmen's Association*. A copy of this newspaper is included in the package of information sent to individuals who respond to our offer to send information about future amendments to the Acts. *Please refer to the back of the book for more information on this offer.*

*Remember, Acts 17 & 66 affect every person in Pennsylvania who currently, or at any time in the future, owns or uses a handgun, rifle or shotgun. If you own a gun or if you intend to acquire one, or if you intend to sell, give or loan one to a child or grandchild, then you need to read this book **and** to obtain the updated information about the amendments to the Acts as they are enacted by the legislature.*

MAJOR GUN-RIGHTS ORGANIZATIONS
AND INFORMATION SOURCES FOR PENNSYLVANIANS

There are many gun-rights organizations in Pennsylvania. In some counties there may be two or three or more. We do not have the space in *this* edition to list every organization but we are considering listing *every* such Pennsylvania and national organization in the *next* edition of this book. So if your organization is not listed here, please write or FAX us with the pertinent information so that we might possibly include it.

National Rifle Association (NRA)
11250 Waples Mill Road
Fairfax, VA 22030
http://www.nra.org/

Gun Owners of America (GOA)
8001 Forbes Place, Suite 102
Springfield, VA 22151
http://www.gunowners.org

Pennsylvania Sportsmen's Association (PSA)
Membership: 1-800-933-5530; P.O. Box 1225, Hermitage, PA 16148
Legislative Committee: FAX 412-538-9406
    e-mail: psa-leg@nauticom.net
Pennsylvania Sportsmen's News: FAX 412-962-0350
    e-mail: psa-psn@nauticom.net
Atty. J. Michael McCormick
Phone: 412-826-1883 FAX: 412-828-7641

Pennsylvania Gun Collector's Association (PGCA)
P.O. Box 341
Bethel Park, PA 15102

Pennsylvania Federation of Sportsmen's Clubs (Federation)
2426 N. 2nd Street
Harrisburg, PA 17110

Firearms Owners Against Crime (FOAC)
P.O. Box 74
Presto, PA 15142
FAX: 412-257-1099; e-mail: http://www.hhi.com\foac\

Allegheny County Sportsmen's League (ACSL)
FAX: 412-882-9115
e-mail: acsl@nauticom.net

Pennsylvania Trappers Association
P.O. Box 567
Fairfield, PA 17320

The War Room - Jim Quinn
http://www.warroom.com

Keystone Firearms Coalition (KFC)
P.O. Box 331
Southampton, PA 18966
Phone & FAX : 215-968-9747; e-mail: adbco@netaxs.com

AirPower Information Services
308 Windermere Ave.
Lansdowne, PA 19050
Northeast U.S.A. H.Q. for Paul Revere Network (PRN)
BBS: 610-259-2193; e-mail; jim.henry@airpower.com

Jews for the Preservation of Firearms Ownership (JPFO)
2872 South Wentworth Avenue
Milwaukee, WI 53207
Phone: 414-769-0760; FAX: 414-483-8435
http://www.mes.net/nlpyleprn/jpfo.html

Pennsylvania Rifle & Pistol Association (PR & PA)
P.O. Box 711
Millville, PA 17846

PART I: QUESTIONS & ANSWERS ABOUT OWNING & USING GUNS IN PENNSYLVANIA

PART I
ANSWERS TO COMMONLY ASKED QUESTIONS ABOUT GUNS IN PENNSYLVANIA

Q. Do I have a *right* to own a gun?

A. Yes. According to article 1, section 21 of the constitution of the Commonwealth of Pennsylvania, *"The right of the citizens to bear arms in defense of themselves and the State shall not be questioned."* However, your right to own or possess a gun (owning is *not* the same as possessing) can be affected by a number of factors including: any criminal activity you may have been involved in, or *accused of*, the type of gun, your age, your mental state, and many other factors. Read this book to find out how these factors affect you.

Q. Will reading all the Pennsylvania statutes (laws) about guns tell me everything I need to know about my rights and responsibilities as a gun owner?

A. No. There are many federal laws which also apply. You must obey the *Pennsylvania laws* and also all the *federal laws*. Generally, the penalties for disobeying federal laws are more severe than those for disobeying similar state laws.

In addition, as we point out in the disclaimer, the legislature *enacts* laws about guns and the courts *interpret* those laws. It is entirely possible that you could read the law, or our comments on the law, as they are printed in this book, and conclude that something you are thinking of doing is perfectly lawful, only to find out afterwards that the courts have interpreted or expanded the law to make what you are thinking of doing, in fact, *un*lawful. Read the disclaimer again for a complete explanation of what this book tells you . . . and what it doesn't. Of course, your lawyer should be able to help you. If he is unable to help, however, you can call the NRA Attorney Referral Program (phone: 703-267-1250) for a local attorney, if you are an NRA member.

Q. In the last Q & A you mentioned state and federal laws. What about local laws? The municipality I live in just passed an ordinance that prohibits anyone from keeping a total of more than five rifles, shotguns or handguns in their home and I have a total of eight. Must I get rid of three of my guns?

A. *Local* laws may be applicable in rare instances (for example: someone who has recently built a shooting range, the noise from which constitutes a public nuisance); but § 6120 of Title 18, recently revised, explicitly prohibits any county, municipality or township from regulating (among other things) the lawful ownership of firearms. Referred to by some as the "pre-emption" statute; it simply means that the power to regulate firearms and ammunition rests *exclusively* with the state; and its statutes supersede those of any local government. The ordinance you mentioned is invalid.

This same statute (18 Pa. C.S. § 6120) was used to overturn a City of Pittsburgh ordinance prohibiting the sale of semi-automatic pistols whose magazines ("clips") held more than ten rounds of ammunition. In 1996 the Pennsylvania Supreme Court, in a 4-1 decision, affirmed that although the state constitution gave municipalities the right to adopt home-rule charters, a local government's authority was limited by both the state constitution and laws passed by the Legislature. In a stinging rebuke to lawmakers in Pennsylvania's two largest cities (Philadelphia and Pittsburgh), who had passed gun control laws, the court said (as excerpted from their decision):

> "Article 1, Section 21 of the Constitution of Pennsylvania provides: 'The right of the citizens to bear arms in defense of themselves and the State shall not be questioned.' Because the ownership of firearms is constitutionally protected, its regulation is a matter of statewide concern. The constitution does not provide that the right to bear arms shall not be questioned in any part of the commonwealth except Philadelphia and Pittsburgh, where it may be abridged at will, but that it shall not be questioned in any part of the commonwealth."

This is probably a good place to advise the reader that in Pennsylania there are almost no sanctions to discourage local municipal or law enforcement officials from creating regulations or interpreting (perhaps we should say, *mis*interpreting) statutes in impermissible ways. If you run afoul of such a situation and are arrested or fined, the court may eventually find that you were in the right - but only after a significant and unrecoverable expenditure for legal fees on your part. The responsible local officials are not likely to be reprimanded; and if defeated in court, may immediately seek new, more creative ways to harass the next hapless gun owner. *So, be aware that having the law on your side does not mean that some degree of caution in your activities isn't required.* In the event local authorities or police seize your guns, refer to the Q & A at pages 50-52 of this book. (Note that *recent* developments indicate that where a pattern of abuse by public officials can be shown, there is the possibility of bringing suit for violations of civil rights, with the prospect of collecting both damages and costs of litigation.)
[See 18 Pa. C.S. § 6120 in this book.]

Q. In the last Q & A you mentioned shooting ranges and noise. A bunch of high priced houses were recently built about a half mile away from our range; and now the owners are complaining that the noise from our range is disturbing them. Our borough council says we will have to restrict

our shooting hours, or maybe even shut down. I doubt that we have the money to fight these people. Is there anything we can do?

A. Yes, there certainly is something you can do. In 1988 the Pennsylvania Legislature passed a law which stated that shooting ranges and similar facilities were exempt from civil and criminal prosecution in any matter relating to noise or noise pollution, so long as those facilities are currently in compliance with any noise related statutes that existed *at the time construction on the range began.* Simply check the lawbooks of your municipality to find out what noise related laws were on the books at that time . . . and those are the only noise related laws that you are required to obey. Dennis Pavlik, of the *Westmoreland County Sportsmen's Association,* who has had experience with such problems suggested that continued harrassment could possibly allow you to file suit for civil rights violations or even malicious prosecution; check with an attorney. *[See 1988, P.L. 452, No. 74, § 1 in this book.]*

Q. **I started looking at Part II, the Pennsylvania statutes (laws) relating to guns, and I am really confused. It seems as though every few pages there's a new definition for the same word. I see "firearms" defined as *not including* rifles and shotguns, and then "firearms" defined as *definitely including* rifles and shotguns. And I see other words which seem to be very similar - such as "weapons," "offensive weapons" and . . . . What's going on?**

A. The Pennsylvania statutes reproduced in Part II were enacted during a 145 year period starting in 1850! In *each statute*, lawmakers used certain definitions and terms; and as you might guess, those definitions and terms changed over the years. Also, *within each statute* several different definitions for the same word may have been used.

Below you will find a list of words that relate to guns and weapons in general. All but the last two appear in Title 18, which is the primary package of Pennsylvania statutes that regulate handguns and other weapons. The section in which each definition appears is listed so that you can check the definitions. Refer to Part III: Statute Index, to find the statutes and see how the definitions change from section to section.

All references are to Title 18 (which means that "18 Pa. C.S." precedes each § number) except the last two in the right hand column.

firearm [§ 6102]	deadly weapon [§ 2301]
antique firearms [§ 6118]	weapon [§ 5122 (b) (2)]
instrument of crime [§ 907]	firearm [§ 5515 (a)]
weapon [§ 907]	air rifles [§ 6304 (g)]
offensive weapon [§ 908]	firearm [34 Pa. C.S. § 102]
weapon [§ 912]	firearm [42 Pa. C.S. § 9712 (e)]

The purpose of providing this list (which is **not** all inclusive) is to show that there **are different definitions** of what might appear to be the same thing. Note, for example, that there are five definitions of firearms listed above. How do you know what definition applies to you? It's simple in most cases. You look at the **section** that applies to your particular situation. The definition within that section is the definition that applies to you.

When you see the word, "firearm" without a reference anywhere in the statute to a specific definition, you may reasonably assume that the definition intended is the "default definition," which is the definition from 18 Pa. C.S. § 6102 - which is essentially the definition of a handgun.

Bear in mind, however, one extremely important comment made in the disclaimer. The legislature **enacts** laws, the courts **interpret** them. It is entirely possible that a section, which as a **hypothetical example**, might define a "gun" as a device that fires a projectile, may have been interpreted by the courts to include air rifles, and electrical devices such as Tasers®. *So, be aware that any court decision ("case law") can change the way the law is interpreted in the future.*

To make life more confusing, you should understand that a decision issued by, say, a judge of the Allegheny County Court of Common Pleas is not binding on any other Allegheny Court of Common Pleas judge, nor is it binding on any judge of the Courts of Common Pleas of any of Pennsylvania's other 66 counties. And, further (depending on the exact situation), decisions of the Courts of Common Pleas can be appealed to Superior Court, whose decisions, in turn, can be appealed to the Pennsylvania Supreme Court (whose decisions are binding on all lower courts). So, now you should better understand why it is so important to contact an attorney knowledgeable about gun laws in the event you are charged with a gun law violation.

Q. The gun shops in my town have a relatively limited selection of guns; but there's a new store in a nearby state that has a huge selection. Can I drive over and buy my guns from them?

A. To answer that question we must look at *all* the possibilities . . . because there is a *different* answer for each possibility.

By federal law you may not buy a firearm of any kind, not even a rifle or shotgun, from an *individual* in another state. To legally arrange a purchase from another state which you cannot make yourself, you may ask for the guns to be delivered to a dealer in the other state, who will ship them to a dealer in Pennsylvania. You can then acquire the guns from the Pennsylvania dealer who will transfer the gun to you in accordance with Pennsylvania and federal laws.

If you desire to purchase a gun from an out-of-state *dealer* - that is, someone with a Federal Firearms License (FFL) - then the answer to this question depends on a number of factors, as detailed on the next page.

If the gun you want is a *handgun*, then federal law prohibits the dealer from selling it to you directly. You must have it shipped to a Pennsylvania dealer by the out-of-state dealer; you may only buy handguns in your state of residence.

If the gun you want is a *long gun*, and the dealer is in a *contiguous* (neighboring) state (for example, Ohio or West Virginia), and you make the purchase *before January 1, 1997,* you may purchase the gun in accordance with the laws of the neighboring state, and of Pennsylvania (18 Pa. C.S. § 6141), which allows long gun purchases in contiguous states), transport it to Pennsylvania, and own it legally in Pennsylvania.

If the situation is exactly as described in the paragraph just above, but the state is *not a contiguous state*, a curious thing happens. The federal Gun Control Act of 1968 permitted purchases of rifles and shotguns (but not handguns) in *contiguous* states (if allowed by reciprocal agreements between the states). A later federal statute (the McClure-Volkmer Act of 1986) expanded that right to purchases from *any and all states,* when the purchase is made in accordance with all applicable laws of both states. (The reason for the change was that many sportsmen needed to be able to purchase rifles and shotguns in non-contiguous states for lawful activities such as hunting and competitive meets.) But being able to *purchase* a gun in another state does not mean that you are allowed to *take it back* to Pennsylvania. And, in fact, until January 1, 1997, a Pennsylvania resident is allowed to purchase a long gun in a non-contiguous state, in accordance with the federal McClure-Volkmer Act. But, based on an interpretation of Pennsylvania's contiguous state statute (18 Pa. C.S. § 6141, mentioned above) by the Pennsylvania State Police, the buyer is *not* currently permitted to bring the long gun back into Pennsylvania. The interpretation is not definitive and work is afoot to change that interpretation so that Pennsylvania long gun buyers will be able to legally bring rifles and shotguns purchased in non-contiguous states back into Pennsylvania.

After January 1, 1997, it gets even trickier. The McClure-Volkmer Act, which is the federal law that enables an out-of-state dealer to sell a long gun to a Pennsylvania resident (or any non-resident), requires that the dealer have *"actual knowledge"* that they are complying with the laws of the non-resident buyer's home state (in our case, Pennsylvania). Now, Pennsylvania's Acts 17 & 66, require that after January 1, 1997, a background check be made on any Pennsylvania resident who wishes to purchase a rifle or shotgun. That's easy for a Pennsylvania dealer - Pennsylvania law spells out exactly how it is to be done. But, the out-of-state dealer - even a dealer in a contiguous state - has no way of making a proper background check. Furthermore, the out-of-state dealer, being well aware of the confusion of Pennsylvania's new gun laws, will have no way of knowing if he/she is in compliance with *all* of them. If the out-of-state dealer cannot be certain he is complying with *all* of Pennsylvania's gun laws, he does not have *"actual knowledge"* that he is doing so . . . and is risking a federal felony charge by making the sale. Hence, an out-of-state dealer is unlikely to risk his business . . . or his freedom . . . by making the sale. Thus, Acts 17 and 66 may effectively prevent Pennsylvanians from purchasing rifles and shotguns out-of-state.

At the beginning of the last paragraph we said that the business of buying guns in other states was getting "trickier." If you think the last paragraph sounded "tricky," wait until you read what follows.

In mid-1966, Harry Schneider, *Legislative Chairman* of the *Pennsylvania Sportsmen's Association,* and attorney, J. Michael McCormick, queried the BATF about the situation described in the last paragraph - that because out-of-state dealers could not perform the background check on Pennsylvania residents, as mandated by Pennsylvania law, they would not be in compliance with Pennsylvania law; and so the federal McClure-Volkmer Act made it illegal for them to sell long guns to Pennsylvanians.

In response to this query, the BATF *[federal Bureau of Alchohol, Tobacco and Firearms]* issued a written opinion that Act 17 **does** seem to impose requirements that would prevent dealers in other states from legally selling rifles and shotguns to Pennsylvania residents as of January 1, 1997. After receiving this opinion, Harry Schneider, and Howard Wolfe, Area (Western Pennsylvania) Supervisor of the BATF, met at a gun show for several hours and reviewed both the state and federal statutes.

Schneider explained to Wolfe, that he had discussed this matter with the individuals who drafted the new law and with the Pennsylvania State Police; and they all agreed verbally that it was not their intent to impose restrictions on the ability of Pennsylvanians to buy long guns in other states. The BATF's Wolfe responded by stating that while Act 17 could be interpreted to deny Pennsylvanians the right to buy long guns in other states, *it is not the desire of the BATF to interpret Pennsylvania law in a manner that is more restrictive than the Pennsylvania State Legislature intended.*

Wolfe also indicated that it was his understanding that it was the opinion of the Pennsylvania State Police that the authority of the Commonwealth ended at its borders . . . and so out-of-state dealers did not have to obey Pennsylvania's law requiring a background check; and thus could legally sell long guns to Pennyslvanians.

Wolfe made the further point that the drafters of the Pennsylvania law, in referring to the entities that were selling long guns and which were required to perform the background check, used the phrase: "licensed importers, licensed manufacturers and licensed dealers." The licenses referred to, indicated Wolfe, were state issued licenses, not federally issued licenses. (To be allowed to sell firearms, sellers must obtain **both** federal and state licenses.) Thus, it was **logical** to say that the requirements to obey Pennsylvania's Act 17 ended at the Pennsylvania border, and out-of-state sellers need not obey that law.

Wolfe told Schneider that the BATF was drafting a letter to the Pennsylvania State Police concerning their interpretation of the laws. Once the answers were received by BATF, and if the answers confirm that the Pennsylvania State Police believe that the Pennsylvania Legislature did not intend to restrict the rights of Pennsylvanians to purchase long guns in other states, then the BATF would very possibly reverse their earlier written opinion; and as a result, Pennsylvanians will be allowed to continue to buy long guns in other states after January 1, 1997.

"So," you, the reader, will probably comment after reading the above, *"that seems pretty straightforward. The Pennsylvania State Police and the ATF will probably agree that Pennsylvanians should have the right to purchase long guns in other states. And everyone will agree to interpret the laws so that we can do that. Where's the "really tricky" part you referred to a few paragraphs ago?"*

The really tricky part comes as follows. The rationale that the background check portion of Pennsylvania law need not be obeyed beyond Pennsylvania's borders results from the interpretation by the Pennsylvania State Police that the Legislature was referring to a *Pennsylvania* license when they used the words, "licensed importers ... manufacturer . . . dealers." *The problem is that Pennsylvania does not issue licenses to anyone but dealers.* They do not license importers or manufacturers. But, it is also *possible* that the Legislature *may* have been referring to state licensed dealers who are located in Pennsylvania, since *federally* licensed manufacturers and importers would also have a *state* license to expedite routine transfers.

What about that *new* written opinion that BATF has indicated it would consider issuing, should the Pennsylvania State Police confirm that the intent of the Legislature was not to prohibit out-of-state long gun purchases by Pennsylvanians? Unfortunately, that opinion is exactly what it's titled - an *opinion.* It's a well intentioned opinion; and the BATF should be applauded for their efforts to determine legislative intent and not to impose regulations that are more restrictive than the Legislature's intent. But remember that it is not the BATF or the Pennsylvania State Police, but rather the courts, which will make the ultimate decision as to what this part of the law really means.

How can Pennsylvanians prevent a potentially lengthy court battle at some future date, when recollections of intent are dimmed by the passage of time, and the likelihood of winning the battle for out-of-state long gun purchases is substantially reduced? Very simply: rewrite the law so as to *forever eliminate the question of legislative intent.* A good way to do that is through the "Grass Roots Reforms," mentioned earlier.

Ammunition may be bought or sold without regard to state boundries; but see a subsequent Q & A to determine the minimum age requirement for purchasing various types of ammunition. The applicability of the information in this answer is contingent on all parties obeying whatever state and federal laws are in existence at the time of the purchase or transfer.

The only exception to the federal laws prohibiting the sale, transfer, delivery or transportation of firearms from individuals in one state to individuals in another, is in the case of firearms received by bequest or intestate succession (a fancy legal phrase which means: someone died and didn't have a will; so, because of your relationship to the deceased, certain items they owned now become yours). However, there are *exceptions to this exception*; so if you are in this situation, be certain to check with an attorney.
[Federal law; 18 Pa. C.S. § 6141, § 6111.1.4 in this book.]

Q. **I am going to be moving to another state. How do I get my guns from the state in which I am now residing to the state in which I am going to be residing, other than in my personal vehicle?**

A. Federal law allows you to pack your guns in with your household goods when changing your residence to another state and using a moving company. You must notify the mover that the shipment includes guns. Be aware that some states may prohibit certain types of guns that are legally owned by you in the state in which you currently reside. Be sure to obtain approval, in advance *(and in writing)* before the guns leave your state.

Q. **I like to do target shooting and hunting and will be traveling to Texas where I will stay with friends who own a target range. I will be traveling through many states, counties and cities, all with their own gun laws. How do I get my guns from Pennsylvania to Texas without risking arrest if my vehicle is stopped and searched in a municipality in which I am not allowed to have a gun?**

A. Surprisingly enough (but only after a lot of "nudging" from the NRA) Uncle Sam has come to your rescue. If you are traveling by *motor vehicle* between states, you are entitled to transport firearms (rifles, shotguns and handguns) *for sporting purposes from a place* where you are allowed to possess and transport them, *to any other place* where you are allowed to possess and transport them, if the firearms are unloaded and locked in the trunk; or if there is no trunk, in a locked container other than the glove compartment or console. Bear in mind that you must be allowed to lawfully *possess and transport both in your origin state and in your final destination state.*

Of course, matters are not quite so simple if you are *flying.* Federal law prohibits your carrying any firearm, concealed or not concealed, on or about your person, or in carry-on baggage, while aboard a *commercial* aircraft. To transport your firearms under these circumstances you must deliver the unloaded firearm into the custody of the airline (or of any common carrier or contract carrier) for the duration of the trip.

According to Federal Aviation Regulation 108.11 and discussions with an official of the FAA, you may alternatively put your unloaded gun(s) into checked baggage (to which you would have no access while in transit). Do it this way. Put your unloaded (but not necessarily disassembled) guns into a hardshell case. Go to an inside ticket counter (not a curbside check-in) and declare the contents; the agent may then put a tag on the *inside* of the case. Airport personnel have the right to examine the guns to confirm that they are, indeed, unloaded. Ammunition must be in a locked container and packaged so that the primers are protected. Both manufacturers' factory packaging and after market ammunition boxes satisfy this concern.

As pointed out in another Q & A most commercial airports are posted against entry with a concealed weapon. To ensure that you encounter no problems, contact someone with the appropriate authority at the airport before leaving your home, advise them of what you are about to do, and confirm that there will be no problem in entering the building with your guns packed as described above. Carry with you a piece of paper on which you have written the name and phone number of the person you spoke with, plus the date and time of the call, in case there is any "problem" when you arrive at the ticket counter.
[Federal law.]

Q. I'm not driving to another state and I'm not so sure I want to put my guns on an airplane. Can I just ship them?

A. Yes, but certain federal laws apply. If you are *hunting*, you may ship the firearm to yourself, in care of another person, in another state. The person to whom you ship the guns should *not* open the package and instead should hold it until your arrival and only *you* should open it. Be sure that you are allowed to possess and use the guns in the locale to which you are shipping them.

There are two primary methods for shipping guns: U.S. Mail, and common or contract carrier. Refer to the next Q & A for details on what methods you may use for shipment.

Q. I have some guns that have not been used recently. One of them needs repair; and I would like to have another one modified. Can I just pack them up and send them to the manufacturer, or to a gunsmith to have the work done?

A. Federal law will likely apply in these cases. (Remember that the word "firearms," in most federal laws, refers collectively to rifles, shotguns and handguns.)

According to federal law, *rifles* and *shotguns* that *you own* can be *mailed* (using the U.S. Postal Service) or *shipped*, from *your state* to *dealers* and *manufacturers* (but no one else) in *any other state*, for any lawful purpose including sale, repair, or customizing. A dealer is someone who has a Federal Firearms License (FFL). If you ship to a gunsmith in another state be sure the gunsmith has an FFL or else both you and the gunsmith will be in violation of federal law. (Remember, an individual - someone who is not a dealer - cannot ship firearms to another individual in another state). You may do the same with handguns as you do with rifles and shotguns, except that you *may not* use U.S. Mail; you must use some other method of shipment.

Be sure to check with any shipping company you might use for shipping your guns; some shipping companies may not accept firearms. Furthermore, federal laws govern shipments by shipping companies you might use, which are known as "common carriers." (Common carriers you may have heard of include UPS, RPS, Federal Express, Airborne Express, Purolator Courier, Greyhound Package Express and many others.)

Federal law requires that if you deliver a firearm (rifle, shotgun or handgun) to a common carrier, that the shipment must be accompanied by a written notice to the carrier of the contents of the shipment. The carrier is prohibited from marking the shipping carton in any way that indicates that there's a gun inside. Remember, be sure to contact the carrier *before* you make final arrangements for shipping any firearm.

Q. I am traveling to another state, to go hunting for small game. Can I legally borrow or rent a gun in the other state?

A. Yes. Federal law permits you to borrow or rent a rifle, shotgun or handgun in another state for *sporting purposes.* Of course, you will still have to meet all the requirements that exist in the locales - municipality, county and state - in which you are borrowing or renting and using the firearm. Note that the 5 day waiting period described in a subsequent Q & A would apply unless that state had implemented the instantaneous background check.

Q. I see from the previous question that I am allowed to loan or rent a handgun for sporting purposes according to federal law. Can I loan or rent a gun in Pennsylvania for any other purpose - say, for example, to a friend who needs to carry a gun for protection?

A. Before Act 17 was enacted § 6115 of Title 18 was sometimes interpreted as making it illegal to *lend* or *give* your firearm to anyone else. This section was included in an attempt to control "gun sharing," a problem that had become rampant in Pittsburgh and Philadelphia. (One or more guns would be passed around to gang members to be used when needed for robberies and shootings.) The problem was that there was potential for law abiding sportsmen to be prosecuted for loaning their guns to others for hunting or other such purposes.

Act 17 reduced this potential problem by listing a broad group of exceptions to the prohibition against loaning guns. Read that section to understand what you can, and cannot do; but note that the matter of loaning a "firearm" to a minor is not addressed - thus possibly allowing prosecution of an adult who gives a handgun to a minor in the minor's home and walks beyond the area within which he can "supervise" the minor. *[See 18 Pa. C.S. § 6115 in this book.]*

Q. At what age can I own or use a gun?

A. That's a much more involved question than you think. It depends on the kind of gun and how it is to be used. Here are the details.

Purchasing, owning or possessing a starter pistol . . . 18 yrs.
(It is illegal to *sell* a starter pistol to anyone under
the age of 18. But, it is legal to *use* a starter pistol
for an athletic, dramatic or similar event at any age)
[See 18 Pa. C.S. § 6303 in this book]

Purchasing an air rifle . . . . 18 yrs.
(It is illegal to *sell* an air rifle to anyone under
the age of 18. Special provisions allow youths
younger than 18 to *own*, *use* or *possess* an air
rifle or other "gun" that expels a pellet.)
[See 18 Pa. C.S. § 6304 in this book.]

Using (but not buying) any type of firearm,. . . 12-14 yrs.
including a handgun, rifle or shotgun, to take, hunt
or trap game or wildlife when accompanied by
someone at least 18 years of age who is a parent,
family member, guardian or someone serving as
parent in their absence (in loco parentis).
[See 34 Pa. C.S. § 2711 in this book.]

As above, but accompanied by *someone* 18 years . . 14-16 yrs.
or older who is not a parent, family member,
guardian or someone serving in loco parentis.
[See 34 Pa. C.S. § 2711 in this book.]

As above, but *not* acompanied by another . . 16-18 yrs.
person 18 years or older.
[See 34 Pa. C.S. § 2711 in this book.]

Carrying a .22 caliber rimfire rifle or handgun . . . no
while trapping furbearers, and accompanied by an   minimum
adult licensed furtaker at least 18 years of age.   age
[See 34 Pa C.S. § 2363, § 2704 (c) (3) in this book.]

Carrying a handgun while hunting, taking fur- . . . 18 yrs.
bearers, fishing, or training dogs, if licensed for
that activity and if in possession of a sportsman's
firearm permit.
[See 18 Pa. C.S. § 6106 in this book.]

Borrowing a handgun, if under the supervision of . . . no
anyone 21 years or older. Note that "supervision"   minimum
generally requires "proximity" - the minor must be   age
within voice and/or vision range of the adult.
[See 18 Pa. C.S. § 6110.1, § 6115, in this book.]

Possessing or transporting a handgun. Note that . . . 18 yrs.
the individual must be in compliance with other
sections of the law while possessing or transporting (e.g.
unloaded, not concealed unless a lawful exception, etc.)
[See 18 Pa. C.S. § 6110.1 in this book]

Purchasing a rifle or shotgun. . . . . 18 yrs.
[See 18 Pa. C.S. § 6302 in this book.]

Purchasing ammunition for a rifle or shotgun. . . . 18 yrs.
[See 18 Pa. C.S. § 6302 in this book.]

Purchasing a handgun. . . . . 21 yrs.
[Federal Law.]

Purchasing ammunition for a handgun. . . . . 21 yrs.
[Federal law.]

Obtaining a license to carry a concealed handgun.. . 21 yrs.
[See 18 Pa. C.S. § 6109 (b) in this book.]

Q. I see the age of 18 popping up several times in the previous question. I heard that the section in the old Uniform Firearms Act (§ 6110) that had to do with possession of a gun by persons under 18 years of age was repealed. Is that true? Why was it repealed? What was it replaced with?

A. A well-intentioned section of Act 17 was written to eliminate the problem of juveniles with criminal intent having handguns. To distinguish it from the old § 6110, which was repealed, the new section was denoted § 6110.1 and its specific purpose was to keep guns out of the hands of minors (youths under the age of 18) who should not have them, while at the same time, giving legal access to guns by minors for lawful purposes *when appropriately supervised.* The legislators titled the section "Possession of Firearm by Minor" to emphasize the focus and importance of this part of Act 17.

In a nutshell, § 6110.1 allows minors access to guns for activities such as hunting, trapping and target shooting while under the supervision of certain classes of adults. Unfortunately the new law still leaves many questions about gun possession by a minor unanswered.

Here's an example. The *legal* definition of "possession" is different from the *ordinary* or dictionary definition. To *laymen* a minor would be "in possession" of a gun when it was in the minor's hands. To *the law*, a minor could be "in possession" of a gun in his house, *if the gun were in any way accessible to the minor when the parents walked out of the house, even if for just a few seconds.* (This is known as "constructive possession".) This is not a totally hypothetical situation; in a recent decision a federal judge found an adult was in "possession" of a handgun when the adult was downstairs answering the door, and the gun was in a zippered bag in an upstairs closet. A Pennsylvania judge could follow the lead *(precedent)* of the federal judge and rule the same way.

Is there a defense against a charge of "constructive possession"? Actually, in Pennsylvania, there is. The term "possession" is defined in the Crimes Code, 18 Pa. C.S. § 301 (c), in its preliminary provisions, relating to culpability, rather than to firearms. According to the Code, "possession is an act, within the meaning of this section, if the possessor knowingly procured or received the thing possessed or was aware of his control thereof for a sufficient period to have been able to terminate his possession." Thus, a person accused of violating Pennsylvania law because of "constructive possession" of a gun, who was not aware that he/she actually "possessed" it, might have a valid defense in a Pennsylvania court.

Here's another example of a potential problem with Act 17. Consider the following actual event that occurred in Texas. Three young girls were alone in a house. They observed several men slitting the window screens with knives and entering the house, putting the girls into great danger. One of the girls, knowing where her father kept his handgun got the gun and shot and killed one of the intruders as he was about to grab her.

Back in the 70's, when this happened, both the father and the girl were applauded for their actions. Today, in Pennsylvania under Act 17, here's what could happen.

The father (and the mother?) could be arrested for willfully and intentionally making a gun available to these minor children in violation of Act 17 ("actual possession").

Now, common sense should dictate that the district attorney refuse to prosecute - but some district attorneys are motivated more by the prospect of headlines than by the administration of justice. And common sense should also dictate that a jury refuse to convict - but many juries are not informed that the United States Supreme Court has upheld the common law right of juries to find a defendent innocent if the law is unjust or the violation is "technical."

So, assuming that the district attorney prosecutes and the jury finds the parent(s) guilty, then even if the judge gives the parent a suspended sentence, all does not bode well.

Based on the maximum penalty that **could have been given,** the parent(s) have now been put into a class of people prohibited from owning a firearm, both by Pennsylvania law, and by federal law. They now have no way to protect themselves from the friends and relatives of the intruders who may decide to wreak vengeance on the entire family. And should a loving grandmother decide to help the family by giving them a gun so that the father could defend the girls against attack, the grandmother would be guilty of a third degree felony, subjecting her to a jail term of up to 7 years. A second offense subjects grandma to a jail term of up to 10 years with a **mandatory** minimum of 5 years. Even if the district attorney refused to prosecute, grandma could be sent to jail under federal statutes.

This is not, as they say, a pretty picture. But as state and federal laws currently stand, such a situation is a very real possibility. Subsequent technical amendments could "fix" Pennsylvania's Act 17; but federal laws could still cause the problems described above.
[See 18 Pa. C.S. § 301 (c), § 6110.1, § 6111 (g) (2) and (h) (1) in this book.]

Q. Well, now that you've brought up the matter of intruders, please explain what I am allowed - or forbidden - to do if an intruder should enter my home.

A. You have probably heard the saying, "A man's home is his castle." That phrase sums up many of the laws concerning self-defense in your home; they traditionally gave you the right to defend yourself or others in your home, by using deadly force, without the need to retreat to other rooms or flee your home.

A potential problem arose in the past, in that some of the laws could be interpreted to allow you to use deadly force only for the defense of lives and not for defense of property. So, if you were in a situation where someone entered your home, and you used deadly force against them, you might be required to stand trial to "prove" that lives were in danger.

In 1980 (and later, by revision, in 1981), Pennsylvania legislators decided to ensure that every citizen of the Commonwealth had a right to defend their home without first playing a game of *"Twenty Questions"* with an intruder to determine whether the intruder were after their property or their lives. Thus, legislators passed Act 235 of 1980 which specified that if your dwelling were entered, and if you had no reason to believe that the entry was lawful, and that if you had no reason to believe that less than deadly force would be adequate to terminate the entry, that you could use deadly force. You do not have to see a weapon or hear a threat of bodily harm to make that presumption. And you do not have to warn the intruder or otherwise lay yourself open to potential harm by making your presence known. And the entry does not have to occur after dark.

What you **cannot do**, is use deadly force on intruders **before** they enter your home. For example, someone standing on your porch, screaming threats at you, warrants a call to the police but **not** a shotgun blast through the screen door. You also cannot use deadly force against an intruder who may have **been** in your home but who is **now** in retreat outside your home, with certain possible exceptions involving forcible felonies committed while previously in your home.

As explained by Allegheny County District Attorney Robert Colville, the presumption that any intruder in your home is prepared to inflict grievous bodily harm is "rebuttable" - fancy legal talk for: the police, the coroner and the district attorney's office will examine all aspects of the ocurrence before the district attorney declares it a "justifiable homicide."

Situations in and around your house, in which shooting another person will likely *not* be declared a justifiable homicide . . . and in which you will likely *stand trial for murder*, include, but are by no means limited to:

A confrontation on the sidewalk in front of your house, with a person who is unarmed, or armed with a weapon which he could not use against you if you retreated inside your house. *(You have a duty to retreat inside your house to avoid using deadly force.)*

A confrontation on a porch or deck or other **un**enclosed part of your house, with a person who is unarmed, or armed with a weapon he could not use against you if you retreated inside your house. *(The same comment applies here as above - you have a duty to retreat into your house to avoid using deadly force.)*

Shooting a person in the back, whether inside or outside your house, as he attempts to flee with stolen goods. (You are not defending yourself or another against mortal [life threatening] danger; you are trying to stop the theft of property, for which you are not allowed to use deadly force.)

Shooting an inebriated neighbor who stumbles into your house by mistake and who is clearly not a danger to you or your family.

Q. I am 34 years old and want to buy a gun. I was a bit "rambunctious" when I was younger. As they say in the song, *"I fought the law, but the law won."* How will this affect my ability to purchase that gun?

A. There are two sets of laws that determine whether you can purchase *any* kind of gun (handgun, rifle, shotgun): federal law and the new state laws, Acts 17 and 66. Although federal and state laws are somewhat different, they both tend to say the same thing: if you have been convicted of a crime of violence or if you have been involved in any, particularly reprehensible activities - illegal drugs, stalking, and so on - you will probably not be able to own a gun of *any* kind, or even ammunition. And if you already have a gun you could be forced to give it up if the authorities discover it *and* be fined and/or jailed for owning possessing, transferring, using, controlling or selling it.

First, *by federal law*, you are prohibited from owning, possessing, receiving, shipping or transporting *firearms* (rifles, shotguns or handguns) *or ammunition* if you are a member of one of the following prohibited classes of people:

- Those convicted of crimes committed *anywhere*, and punishable by imprisonment for more than one year, except: state misdemeanors (other than those involving a firearm or explosive) punishable by two years or less in prison and certain business related crimes such as anti-trust or unfair trade practices.
- Fugitives from justice.
- Unlawful users of certain depressant, narcotic or stimulant drugs.
- Those adjudicated as mental defectives or incompetents, or those committed to any mental institution.
- Illegal aliens.
- Citizens who have renounced their citizenship.
- Those persons dishonorably discharged from the Armed Forces.
- Persons under a restraining order for harassing, stalking or threatening.
- Employees of any of the above persons who have a gun as part of their employment.

It is important to understand the terminology in these prohibitions. The first one, for example, states: *"Those convicted of crimes punishable by imprisonment for more than one year . . . ."* What that means is that you cannot own a gun if you were convicted of having violated a law which *could* cause you to be imprisoned for more than a year, *even if, in your particular situation, you were actually imprisoned for a year or less, or were not imprisoned at all!* What counts is the *maximum sentence* you *could have been given,* not the sentence you *actually received.*

In addition, any persons *under indictment* for a crime punishable by imprisonment for more than one year are under the same prohibition, although they do not have to give up firearms they already possess unless and until convicted.

A comment is appropriate here. In a conversation with a legal representative of the BATF (the federal government's Bureau of Alcohol, Tobacco and Firearms) an individual asked about an actual incident in which a person had been imprisoned for a crime committed in a foreign country, with laws very different from ours. Would imprisonment for more than a year for a crime in *that country* prohibit that person from owning a firearm in *this country?* The BATF's answer was, "yes." The questioner than became more specific, explaining that the "terrible crime" was providing bibles to the citizens of the Communist Russia. According to the BATF representative, as long as the "crime" was punishable by imprisonment for more than a year it prevented that person from ever owning a firearm in this country unless "relief from disability" (see below) is obtained; the nature of the "crime" was immaterial.

Under limited conditions, "relief from disability" (that is, the elimination of the prohibition against possessing, receiving, shipping or transporting firearms or ammunition) may be obtained from the U.S. Secretary of the Treasury, or through a pardon, expungement, restoration of rights, or setting aside of a conviction.

So, you, the reader, might be inclined to comment that, as unreasonable as the BATF's position might be, at least that person could obtain "relief from disability" from the Secretary of the Treasury. However, Congress has failed to provide funds for that program for several years; and in fact, in October 1996, deleted funds for that program when they finally voted on the budget. What's worse is that the law does not allow an individual to supply their own funding for the necessary investigation, the results of which could allow relief from disability. This creates an "interesting" precedent, in cases where the disability (prohibition from owning a firearm) resulted from a verdict in a foreign court. The precedent: *that a foreign court has the ability to deny an American citizen a fundamental Constitutional right - the right to bear arms.* Apparently aware of this situation, the legislators who formulated Pennsylvania's Act 17, included this phrase in the law:

> *"The court may grant such relief [from disability] if it determines that . . . the Secretary of the Treasury of the United States has relieved the applicant of an applicable disability imposed by federal law . . .* **except that the court may waive this condition if the court determines that the Congress of the United States has not appropriated sufficient funds to enable the Secretary of the Treasury to grant relief to applicants eligible for the relief."**

The only problem with this phrase is the question of which law - federal or state - takes precedence. If you previously violated the law in a manner which puts you in one of the classes that federal law prohibits from owning, possessing . . . a firearm, and you **cannot** get relief from disability from the federal government because of lack of funding, but you **can** get the requirement waived by the **state** government, can the federal government claim that you are still in violation of **federal** law and prosecute you? Technically, they can; but in October 1996 the author was advised by the BATF that they would not - that Pennsylvania's granting of relief would be accepted.

Second, in Pennsylvania you may not **possess, use, control, sell, transfer or manufacture** a firearm (and that includes rifles and shotguns) if you were ever convicted of one of 43 different crimes, committed anywhere (not just in Pennsylvania). Of course, if you were convicted of such a crime it is likely you will have already been eliminated by the federal law just described above.
[See 18 Pa. C.S. § 6105 in this book.]

One final note. It is important, at this point in the book, to remind you, the reader, of some important distinctions that were made in one of the first Q & A's.

When ordinary folk such as you and I, use the word "gun," we could be referring to any **one** of a variety of weapons - a handgun, a rifle or shotgun, a mortar or even one of those giant, ship mounted 21 inch jobs that can blow up an aircraft carrier. Or we could be referring to just a *few* or perhaps **all** - of those weapons, collectively.

But when legislators, attorneys and the judiciary refer to what **we** call "guns," **they** use a different word, usually "firearms." That word, "firearms," has a very specific meaning . . . and that meaning can change **each** time it is used in a different statute, or in a different section of the same statute.

For example, in § 6109 (concealed weapons) and § 6111 (firearm ownership) a "firearm," for all intents and purposes, is a handgun. But in § 6105 (persons prohibited from owning firearms) and 6111.1 (duties of the Pennsylvania State Police), "firearms" refers to handguns, rifles and shotguns, collectively. And in federal laws, "firearms" frequently refers to handguns, rifles and shotguns, collectively, and sometimes also to "silencers" or any "destructive device."

So, the moral of this story is that when you read the statutes, or case law (decisions handed down by the judiciary in actual

cases) or try to determine what statutes apply in your particular situation, you must, repeat, ***must***, know exactly what types of "firearms" are referred to. Attorneys that specialize in gun law know these things; and so, as emphasized in the disclaimer, you must always contact an attorney knowledgeable in gun law when something as important as your right to own and use a gun . . . or your right to be walking around on the street, rather than languishing in prison . . . is concerned.
[Federal law; See 18 Pa. C.S. § 6105 in this book.]

Q. When I purchase a gun in a Pennsylvania gun shop, must I fill out a bunch of forms? Is there waiting period before I can take the gun home? What if I purchase a gun from a private seller or at a gun show; are there still forms to fill out and a waiting period?

A. This is a very confusing matter, made even more so by the changes made to the old gun laws by Act 17, and then, by the changes to Act 17 made by Act 66 just 6 weeks after Act 17 took effect. To make matters even more confusing, Act 66 mandates changes in the law over the next several years. And of course, let us not forget that the laws treat long guns (rifles and shotguns) differently from the way they treat handguns. In this answer we will try to make sense of the laws as they currently stand, and as they will change in the future.

Definition: "Instantcheck." An abbreviation for the instantaneous records (or background) check mandated by the federal "Brady Law" which determines, using computer compiled information, and the potential purchaser's positive identification (such as a photo driver's license) that the purchaser is not in any of seven described classes (for example, fugitives from justice, drug users, illegal aliens, etc.) who are prohibited by federal law from owning, using, possessing, selling, transferring. . . . a gun or ammunition. A determination can be made in just a few minutes or less. If the prospective gun owner is not found to be in a prohibited class, a unique approval number and receipt are generated as proof of the finding and the person is allowed to take possession of the gun. In the Commonwealth of Pennsylvania, the State Police have the responsibility of setting up the Instantcheck system.

LONG GUNS (RIFLES & SHOTGUNS)

- *Purchased from a private party* (someone who is not a dealer in guns and therefore does not have an FFL) *before Instantcheck goes into effect.* No forms of any kind (federal or state). No contact with a law enforcement agency. No waiting period.

- *Purchased from a private party after Instantcheck goes into effect.* No forms of any kind (federal or state). No contact with a law enforcement agency. No waiting period. But substantial civil and criminal liability for the seller if he sells to a person whom he has "reason to believe" may be ineligible to lawfully purchase a gun or who has criminal intent.

- *Purchased from a dealer before January 1, 1997.* A federal form ATF4473 identifying the gun purchased and the purchaser, must be completed. No state forms. No Instantcheck. No waiting period.

- *Purchased from a dealer between January 1, 1997 and the time that the Instantcheck system goes into effect.* A federal form ATF4473 is completed. No Instantcheck. No waiting period. A one page form, known as the application/record of sale, is completed with information about the purchaser but not the gun and mailed to the State Police by first class mail within 14 days of the sale. The State Police conduct a criminal history, juvenile delinquency and mental health background check within 10 days. Presumably, the State Police could send officers to the home of anyone who fails the background check, to confiscate *all* guns and ammunition and arrest the person for illegally acquiring the gun.

- *Purchased from a dealer after the Instantcheck system is in place.* A federal form ATF 4473 is completed. No state forms. No waiting period. Instantcheck is used to tell the dealer whether to approve or deny the purchase. If the instant check computer is down or backed up, you may have to wait up to 48 hours before you can take delivery.

HANDGUNS

- *Purchased from a dealer before Instantcheck goes into effect.* A "Brady Form" is completed and sent to the "chief law enforcement officer" ("CLEO") of the "place of residence of the purchaser" by certified or registered mail, return receipt requested. The CLEO is generally the county sheriff.

The CLEO may conduct a background investigation of the prospective gun purchaser. If a background investigation is performed and the purchaser checks out "OK," the CLEO can contact the dealer immediately, *no matter how few days have passed*. The dealer can then release the handgun as soon as the purchaser completes federal form ATF 4473. If the CLEO does not respond, the gun can be released five business days (the "5 day waiting period") after the CLEO's date of receipt of the Brady Form, as indicated on the U.S. Mail return receipt. (A "business day" is a day that Pennsylvania state offices are open, not a day that the CLEO's offices are open.) In addition, a one page state application/record of sales containing a description of the gun and of the purchaser, is completed, and sent, within 14 days, to the Pennsylvania State Police, by first class mail. *Police officers and those with a Pennsylvania License to Carry a Firearm may take immediate possession.*

- *Purchased from a dealer after Instantcheck goes into effect.* A federal form 4473 is completed. In addition, a one page state application/record of sale, containing a description of the gun and of the purchaser is completed, and sent, within 14 days, to the Pennsylvania State Police by first class mail. Instantcheck is used to tell the dealer whether to approve or deny the purchase. The legislative intent is that there be no waiting period, unfortunately, due to a drafting error, the pre-Act 17 48 hour waiting period may be reinstated. Further, if the instant check computer is down or backed up, you may be required to wait up to 48 hours before you can take delivery.

- *Purchased from a private party before Instantcheck goes into effect.* Seller and his gun and purchaser meet at a dealer or offices of the Pennsylvania State Police and follow the procedure described in "Purchased from a dealer before Instantcheck goes into effect," above. Dealer or State Police retain handgun until approval is given or 5 day waiting period passes. Dealer may charge extra for this service.

- *Purchased from a private party after Instantcheck goes into effect.* Seller and his gun, and purchaser, meet at a dealer or offices of State Police and follow the procedure described in "Purchased from a dealer after Instantcheck goes into effect," above. Dealer may charge extra for this service.

Here's a final important note. When you read § 6111 [18 Pa. C.S. § 6111 (a) (1)] you will see that the statute specifies only a *48 hour* waiting period. But throughout this last Q & A we have referred to a *5 day* waiting period. The reason for this seeming contradiction is that although Pennsylvania law specifies a 48 hour waiting period, federal law (the Brady Law) specifies a 5 day period. After Instantcheck is put into effect the waiting period should disappear completely; but current interpretations of Act 17 indicate that a 48 hour state mandated waiting period still remains. If Instantcheck ever "goes down" for more than 48 hours, Pennsylvania law specifies that dealers may revert to the procedure which was in effect before Instantcheck. That would be the 5 day waiting period of federal law; or, if the Brady Law is repealed or found unconstitutional, the waiting period would revert back to the 48 hours of § 6111 (a) (1).

Q. **At the beginning of this book you referred to problems with Act 17 and 66 and gave some examples . . . but pointed out that these were not the only problems. Having read the rather complicated procedures for purchasing guns under the new laws, I wonder if there are any other "traps" to watch out for?**

A. There is one potentially major trap that the writers of the Acts claim is unintended . . . and unimportant. But, past experiences with both federal and state enforcement of gun laws indicates that such "minor" matters can, some day in the future, when people forget how "minor" they were supposed to be, become quite *major.* Here is that trap.

Sections 6111 (b) (1) and (1.1), and 6111 (c) state: "[A dealer selling a handgun, rifle or shotgun shall] obtain a completed application/record of sale from the potential buyer or transferee (that's *you*) to be filled out in triplicate, the original copy to be sent to the Pennsylvania State Police . . . one copy to be retained by the [dealer] and one copy to be retained by the purchaser or transferee." (Words in square brackets are used by the author to indicate the intent of the statute, without reproducing its lengthy verbiage.)

Note that there is no specified time limit for the keeping of the copies of the application/record of sale by the dealer or the purchaser. Without a specified time limit, the dealer and purchaser must keep the copies forever. The Pennsylvania State Police did not include, in their instructions to dealers, a notification to give copies to purchasers.

What could happen if a Pennsylvania State Police officer, or any authorized law enforcement officer, asked a gun owner or dealer to produce his/her copy of an application/record of sale, and it had not been received by the purchaser, or was lost or discarded a year . . . or ten years ago? Well, that would be a violation of § 6111; and according to the Crimes Code (18 Pa. C.S. § 6119) a violation of any section for which a penalty is not explicitly stated is a misdemeanor of the first degree. Reference to 18 Pa. C.S. § 106, shows that a first degree misdemeanor is punishable by imprisonment of up to five years. So, not being able to comply with that request to produce your copy will subject you to a term of imprisonment of up to five years. And a conviction, even if sentence is suspended, will automatically prevent you from ever owning a gun again (because the sentence you could have been given exceeds the one year maximum allowable by federal law for gun ownership).

Clearly, this problem needs to be addressed; the "Grass Roots Reforms," mentioned earlier, do that.
[See 18 Pa. C.S. § 6111 (b) (1) and (1.1), § 6111 (c), § 6119, § 106 in this book.]

Q. In the previous question you indicated that there is currently a 5 day waiting period for the purchase of a handgun. Is there a time when the 5 day waiting period would not apply?

A. The 5 day waiting period does not apply to law enforcement officers - a standard exception to most gun law restrictions - or to people who currently hold a License to Carry a Firearm or to anyone who presents a written statement, issued by the appropriate authority, that the buyer requires access to a firearm because of a threat to his or her life or to the life of anyone in his or her household. Note, however, that the instantaneous background check would apply to these three classes of people, according to Act 17 as it is currently written.
[See 18 Pa. C.S. § 6111 (f) (3) and (f) (4) in this book.]

Q. I have children (or grandchildren) to whom I would like to give my guns. Is that a problem insofar as the law is concerned?

A. Federal gun laws prohibiting sales or transfer between people *in different states* do not make exceptions for transfers be-

47

tween parents and children or grandparents and grandchildren. Theoretically, those transfers are subject to the same restrictions and requirements as any other transfer, including the requirement of filling out the proper forms, a waiting period (if it is a handgun), and so on. Conversations between the BATF and Harry Schneider indicated that the BATF will not consider a parent/child transfer illegal even though such a transfer would be in technical violation of the law; but nothing was said about grandparent/grandchild transfers. Pennsylvania law, in the form of the new Act 17, now exempts such transfers, as well as transfers between spouses, from all the *state* requirements including the instantaneous background check when the transfer is made *within* the state. Note that transfers between siblings are *not* exempted.
[See 18 Pa. C.S. § 6111 (c) in this book.]

Q. Do the laws regarding handguns refer to every conceivable type of handgun?

A. In general, the answer is yes. Note that there are federal bans on certain handguns, and on certain magazines whose capacity exceeds 10 rounds. These are described later in this book in the Q & A concerning "semi-automatic assault weapons."

Note also that as far as Pennsylvania and federal statutes are concerned, any pistol or revolver with a barrel length of 15 inches or more, or overall length of 26 inches or more, is treated as a rifle or shotgun, not as a handgun.
[See 18 Pa. C.S. § 6102 "Firearm" in this book.]

Q. Do I need any type of license or permit to purchase or own a rifle or shotgun?

A. Other than the forms that you might fill out at the time of purchase or transfer, there are no permits or licenses required to own, use or transport your rifle or shotgun. As long as you

are asking this question, however, it would be wise for you to read two comments. First, as described in another Q & A, you are prohibited from carrying any loaded long guns in a vehicle. (There are exceptions, as you will read, but they likely will not apply to you.) And second, because of the potential criminal liability which could be incurred should you sell a rifle or shotgun to someone who uses it illegally, you, as the seller, might find it wise to go through the Act 17 transfer process - which *does* involve various forms - *because going through that process shields from you from any criminal complaint.*
[See 18 Pa. C.S. § 6111 (d) in this book.]

For the information above to apply, that is, for the gun in question to be considered a rifle or shotgun, its overall length must be 26" or more. The length will be measured when the gun is at its shortest; so if the gun has a folding stock, the length will be measured when the stock is *folded*, a restriction confirmed by the BATF in October 1996.

In addition, a rifle must have a minimum barrel length of 16 inches and a shotgun must have a minimum barrel length of 18 inches. The barrel length is measured from the muzzle of the barrel to the face of the closed action, bolt, or cylinder, whichever is applicable.
[See Pa. C.S. § 6102 "Firearm," in this book.]

If the barrel or overall length of the rifle or shotgun is less than the above, not only will the gun not be treated as a rifle or shotgun for the purposes of various laws, including Pennsylvania gun laws, but in addition may be considered a "prohibited offensive weapon" the possession of which can result in major criminal penalties. *(Example: a shotgun with an overall length of less than 26 inches or a barrel shorter than 16 inches may be considered an illegal "sawed-off shotgun.")*

Readers are cautioned that certain guns, such as the Thompson-

Center Contender, can be readily converted from a handgun to a rifle or shotgun by the addition of a longer barrel and a buttstock. Having both the removeable pistol barrel and the rifle or shotgun stock in place at the same time makes the gun a prohibited weapon. This situation gave rise to a recent court case in which the manufacturer of the Thompson Contender was charged by the U.S. government with selling a prohibited weapon even though the company did not deliver the gun to their dealers in the prohibited configuration; that is with pistol barrel and rifle stock mounted on the frame. The case eventually ended up in the U.S. Supreme Court. The government argued that a *"legal"* gun is *"illegal"* if one possesses the components to quickly convert it into an illegal gun. Justice Sandra Day O'Conner delivered an uncharacteristically blistering response to the government attorney, commenting sarcastically that she owned both a shotgun and a hacksaw; and by the government's reasoning, she was therefore in possession of a sawed-off shotgun and should be arrested and imprisoned. The ruling was overturned.

And finally, remember that the provisions regarding ownership, possession, transportation and use of a rifle or shotgun are dependent on the *age* of the person in question.

Q. On the cover of this book you mention that I could have my guns and personal property confiscated. Who can do that . . . and for what reason?

A. There are many situations in which your guns and other property can be confiscated - that is, taken away from you by the police, the sheriff or the Pennsylvania or federal governments. Sometimes the items will be returned; sometimes they won't be.

For example, note the following:

42 Pa. C.S. § 6801 specifies that any firearms or prohibited offensive weapons seized in connection with a violation of the

Controlled Substance, Drug, Device and Cosmetic Act are to be immediately destroyed.
[See 42 Pa. C.S. § 6801 in this book.]

Title 34, which is the Pennsylvania law pertaining primarily to game and wildlife, requires that any personal property related to a violation of any law which is enforced or administered by the Pennsylvania Game Commission be seized and turned over to the Commission. The "personal property" they refer to includes not only guns, traps and decoys, but also boats and vehicles.
[See 34 Pa. C.S. § 102, § 928, § 2310; and 1929, P.L. 177, No. 175 § 712 in this book.]

In cases of domestic violence or violations of protection from abuse orders, the arresting or investigating officer is required to seize all weapons used by the defendant.
[See 18 Pa. C.S. § 2711, 23 Pa. C.S. § 6108, § 6113 in this book.]

There are other such laws on the books in Pennsylvania. And most everyone is well aware that the federal government seizes millions of dollars worth of boats, airplanes, houses, expensive vehicles . . . and of course, guns . . . every year, from persons who are caught violating drug control and other laws.

Also be aware that civil assets forfeiture laws permit your personal and real property to be confiscated on the mere suspicion that they might have been used in a crime or might be the ill-gotten gain of certain crimes.

Further, police may seize firearms as "derivative contraband" but only if they prove the guns were used in a specific crime.

Finally, be aware that your guns might be seized even though you've done nothing wrong. In some jurisdictions (and, it has been reported, especially in Philadelphia) if your legal firearm is seized by police and you are not at fault (for example, your gun was stolen by a burglar and the police recover it), the authorities will not return your gun to you even if you have a current photo-driver's license and a current License to Carry a Firearm. The gun owner is forced to file a motion for return of property under rule 324 of the Pennsylvania Rules of Criminal Procedure, which requires you to hire a lawyer to represent you in a Common Pleas Court hearing. What's the basis for the refusal to return your gun? It's neither an ordinance nor any specific law; rather, "liability exposure" and "insurance concerns" are cited as the reason for not turning over your gun without a court order.

Of course, under Act 17, such municipal conerns are questionable, at least where the gun owner has a License to Carry. See, e.g., Sections 6111 (d) and 6109 (j) in Part II of this book; Moreover, if you are forced to get a court order, consider having your lawyer seek, as well, an award of reasonable counsel fees.

The moral of this answer is: don't break the law and don't be suspected of breaking the law and you'll get to keep your guns and other personal property. Violate or be suspected of violating the law and you could end up without your car, house or gun, sleeping in a cornfield in Iowa.

Q. **I have been told that in Pennsylvania everyone has the right to carry a concealed weapon to protect themselves. Is that true? If I get a concealed weapons permit or "carry permit" can I carry my hunting knife? Or a shotgun under my coat? Can I carry any type of handgun other than a revolver? Can I carry more than one gun at a time? Is there a special place on my person that I must carry the gun that I conceal? Where should I carry my permit?**

A. Like most people you use the phrases "concealed weapons permit or " or "carry permit." That is logical because many states refer to their permit using those words. However, in Pennsylvania the permit you refer to is called a "License to

Carry a Firearm." It has this name because it applies to "firearms," which are specifically defined in § 6102 of the Pennsylvania Uniform Firearms Act. For all intents and purposes a firearm is a *handgun*. Thus the license *does not* allow you to carry concealed, on your person, or in a vehicle: a rifle, a shotgun, a switchblade knife, brass knuckles . . . or just about anything else which you might call a weapon. In fact, carrying one of these other weapons may be a violation of Pennsylvania law. And - *now read this carefully - being convicted of carrying one of these other weapons could cause you to forever lose the right to own a rifle, shotgun or handgun!* To repeat, the only type of "gun" or "weapon" that your license allows you to carry "concealed" is a "firearm," which, as we indicated above, is a handgun.
[See 18 Pa. C.S. § 6106 in this book.]

The handgun you carry concealed, must, of course, be legal - it cannot be one of the guns prohibited by federal law, as explained in a later Q & A. The handgun can be a revolver or a semi-automatic pistol. You can carry one . . . or two . . . or ten handguns, if you can comfortably conceal all that armament. Of course, a police officer finding you with an extraordinarily large number of handguns concealed on your person may question your mental state . . . which, in turn, could ultimately cause you to lose your license. Note also that you should take care to keep your concealed handgun, *concealed.* "Flashing" it is also a good way to get your license revoked.

There is no particular place on your body you should, or should not, conceal your gun. But be very careful when drawing your handgun from its place of concealment - keep your finger off the trigger until your sights are on the target lest you accidentally lose a finger or toe . . . or some other important part of your anatomy!

Where should you carry your license? According to Pennsylvania law, *"When carrying a firearm concealed about one's person or in a vehicle, an individual licensed to carry a firearm shall, upon lawful demand of a law enforcement officer, produce the license for inspection."* The only place you can carry your license and *always* be able to produce it upon demand is on your person - so you should carry it in your wallet or purse, which should always be with or near you. It might also be helpful to keep the telephone number of an attorney well versed in gun law, in the same place as your license. *[See 18 Pa. C.S. § 6122 in this book.]*

Interestingly enough, although your License to Carry a Firearm permits you to carry a handgun concealed on your person or concealed in your vehicle, you *may not* carry a *loaded* rifle or shotgun in your vehicle even if it is in *plain sight* and *not concealed.* In fact you may not carry *any* loaded "gun" in a vehicle or on your person unless it is a "firearm" as defined in § 6102 - which means the "gun" *must* be a handgun. There are special exceptions to this part of the law as explained in another Q & A.

One final comment about those "loaded" rifles and shotguns that you are not allowed to carry in a vehicle. Remember our comment in the disclaimer that it is the legislature that passes gun laws, but it is the courts that interpret them. Accordingly, in many states, a gun in the passenger compartment with no cartridges in the chamber, cylinder or magazine, but with cartridges which are accessible because they too are in the passenger compartment - is still considered a "loaded" gun. To be certain that you are not accused of carrying "loaded" rifles or shotguns in your vehicle, the usual advice is to lock your guns in the trunk and keep the ammunition in the passenger compartment or other area sufficiently separate from the guns that you would have to stop the vehicle, step outside and unlock the trunk, in order to put them together.

Pennsylvania laws regarding the definition of "loaded" may be somewhat different from the laws of other states. Act 66, which amended Act 17, defines a firearm (using the "default" definition of a firearm, from § 6102, which means, essentially, a handgun) as "loaded," in the following ways.

In the case of a gun with a detachable magazine ("clip"), such as a semi-automatic pistol, the gun is considered *loaded* if the magazine is inserted into the gun or if the unloaded handgun and a loaded magazine are in the same container, such as a target shooter's pistol box. The gun is considered to be *unloaded* if a magazine and the unloaded pistol are in different compartments of a multi-compartment container. If both gun and magazine were "loose" in your vehicle, that vehicle could likely be considered the "compartment" and you could be in violation.

Guns (again, we are speaking basically of handguns, not long guns) which do not have detachable magazines (for example, revolvers) are considered loaded only if the ammunition is actually inserted into the gun. Thus, carrying a revolver and a box of ammunition in that same container we mentioned above when discussing semi-automatic pistols, would *not* put you in violation of the law.

The Game and Wildlife Code (as distinct from the Crimes Code, of which Acts 17 and 66 are a part) defines a loaded gun (either a handgun or long gun) as any gun in which a round is inserted in the chamber or an *attached* magazine. *[See 18 Pa. C.S. § 6102 "Loaded," in this book.]*

Now that we've talked about everything that you can - and cannot - do when carrying a concealed handgun, let's check to be sure you are even allowed to carry it at all. To begin with, carrying a concealed handgun is not considered by the Commonwealth to be a right, it is considered a privilege. You are not entitled to that privilege if you are one of thirteen classes of people enumerated in § 6109 (e) (1), which you can find by looking in the Statute Index of Part III of this book. If you do not fall into one of those prohibited classes, you can go to the sheriff's office (or the office of the chief of police in a first class city, of which there is only one in Pennsylvania - Philadelphia) and fill out an application. The sheriff is required to investigate you and to grant or deny the license within 45 days. If he denies it he must specify the reason for the denial, in writing, by certified mail.

Be aware that in some areas the sheriffs have not been quick to grant licenses to private citizens; and will resort to various delaying tactics such as scheduling an "interview" on a date 3 months after you submitted the application, and then telling you that the 45 days start running from the interview date. Being treated in accordance with the laws of Pennsylvania is your right; do not allow your rights to be trampled. Your license, once issued, is valid for five years and costs only $19. At least 60 days before its expiration the sheriff is required to mail you an application for renewal; but his failure to mail, or your failure to receive, the application, does not relieve you of the responsibility to renew the license.

It is important to note that the law *does not differentiate* between a person whose License to Carry a Firearm expired the previous day, and a convicted felon, getting ready to rob a bank, both of whom are caught with a gun and without a *valid* License to Carry a Firearm. Both are subject to the same penalties if tried and convicted . . . penalties which would prevent the innocent citizen from owning a gun ever again. Gun-rights groups are working to change the law so that innocent forgetfulness will not be so costly.

Q. I have a Pennsylvania License to Carry a Firearm and live in the Western Pennsylvania area. I occasionally travel to Philadelphia; am I allowed to carry my concealed handgun within the city of Philadelphia? Could I obtain a License to Carry a Firearm if I lived in Philadelphia?

Are there any places I may not enter carrying a concealed firearm, even if I do have a License to Carry a Firearm?

A. You may obtain a License to Carry a Firearm (if you meet the requirements) no matter where in Pennsylvania you reside. Prior to the enactment of Act 17, a person living in a "first class city" - and the only first class city in Pennsylvania is Philadelphia - was subject to a requirement to which other residents of Pennsylvania were not: the applicant for the license had to show good reason to fear an injury to their person or property or have any other "proper reasons" for carrying a firearm (handgun) and had to be a "suitable individual" to be licensed. As, you can imagine, a law that vague was open to abuse - and that led to numerous complaints. Now that Act 17 is in effect, residents of Philadelphia should be treated the same as residents of any other part of the state and the city appears to be complying, although there is a substantial backlog.

Once you have the license you may carry your concealed handgun anywhere in the Commonwealth of Pennsylvania, except those places in which the right to carry your gun is specifically prohibited. Usually - but not always - restricted areas are "posted" - a sign on the door or entrance tells you that you may not enter if you are carrying a weapon. When you see such a sign you should assume that the prohibition includes *everyone* with a weapon, including a person with a Pennsylvania License to Carry a Firearm. It could be a major - and very costly - error, to assume the opposite: that your license allows you to enter such an area with a concealed handgun despite the posted sign. You can always check with the authorities at the prohibited location - *before you enter it.*

The only persons permitted to bring a weapon into a *federal facility* are the law officers and federal officials of the types mentioned in the disclaimer, and people carrying guns incident to hunting or other "lawful purpose." While carrying a gun is generally lawful for anyone with a License to Carry a Firearm, we recommend you think twice about putting the law "to the test" by entering any federal building while carrying a concealed handgun, even if you hold a License to Carry a Firearm.

Additionally, there are several other specific prohibitions regarding the carrying of concealed handguns, *whether or not* the carrier holds a Pennsylvania License to a Carry Firearm.

First, you may not bring firearms into a *federal courthouse*. Being caught with a gun in a federal courthouse, with or without a Pennsylvania License to Carry a Firearm subjects you to a term of up to two years of imprisonment. And of course, that conviction would *prohibit you from ever owning a gun of any kind* again. (Refer to the federal law listing classes of people prohibited from owning guns, mentioned earlier.)

Second, Act 17, the new gun law which went into effect on October 11, 1995, has instituted a prohibition on carrying a weapon - including a firearm of any kind - into any *"court facility."* The term "court facility" is very loosely defined so it is important to read this part of the law carefully. There will be warning signs posted on all doors, and there should be "facilities" for checking your firearms (is this beginning to sound like Dodge City?) and there will be exceptions to this law but having a License to Carry a Firearm is *not an exception.* Carrying a handgun into a "court facility" when you hold a License to Carry a Firearm is a summary offense and will probably earn you a conviction for a third degree misdemeanor. So. . . read the law!
[See 18 Pa. C.S. § 913 in this book.]

Third, at an *airport*, you may not bring a gun into an area posted against possession of a weapon and/or where access is controlled by security personnel, nor onto a commercial aircraft, nor may you place, or attempt to place, a loaded gun in your checked baggage. Violating this law subjects you to a fine of up to $25,000 plus imprisonment for up to five years in a federal penitentiary.

To be sure that you do not inadvertently violate the law - at potentially great cost to you - be aware of your surroundings, especially signs! For example, the entire indoor portion of the Pittsburgh International Airport is posted against weapons, with signs printed on every outside door. The same is likely true of many other commercial airports throughout the United States. There are procedures in airports for "checking" your gun; be sure to *call in advance* to get the details. See also the Q & A on page 28 in which we discuss air transportation of guns.

Fourth, in Pennsylvania, it is a violation of the Game and Wildlife Code to carry a firearm of any kind (handgun, long gun) or any device by which wildlife could be killed or taken, even if the wildlife is not shot at, while *"recreational spot-lighting."* Note that there is no exemption for holders of a Pennsylvania License to Carry a Firearm.
[See 34 Pa. C.S. § 2310 in this book.]

Fifth, carrying a concealed firearm is forbidden in *state parks.* Even holders of a License to Carry a Firearm, off-duty Game Commission officers, and off-duty police officers are not permitted to carry concealed firearms in state parks! How did such unreasonable restrictions arise? Section 7506 of the Crimes Code (18 Pa. C.S. § 7506) gives the Department of Environmental Resources, (now renamed, the Department of Conservation and Natural Resources [DCNR]), the Pennsylvania Game Commission, and the Pennsylvania Historical and Museum Commission the right to promulgate rules and regulations governing conduct on Commonwealth property.

The state parks are the responsibility of the DCNR. According to Eugene Giza, of the Bureau of State Parks, which is part of the DCNR, firearms (using the § 6102 "default definition," which is to say, handguns) may be concealed in vehicles or trailers or on your person when you are in a vehicle or trailer, but may not be carried concealed on your person when outside a vehicle or trailer, for general purposes of movement in state parks. "Movement in" state parks includes such activities as walking the trails and going to the washhouse. The prohibition applies to everyone, including police and other officers, unless on duty.

Title 71, the Pennsylvania Administrative Code, gives "state park officers" the right to arrest *anyone,* for *any* violation of the rules and regulations . . . even for violations as innocuous as littering! What could happen to any License holder who might be caught with a concealed firearm because they did not see the posted notices of the prohibition or because they thought that the prohibition did not apply to them? Well, § 7506 specifies that any violation of any of the rules and regulations is a summary offense. So the penalty would be relatively minor, compared to the penalty if it were classified as a more serious offense - a misdemeanor or felony - either of which could result in fines, imprisonment, and the possible loss of the right to own firearms. Nevertheless, violating this regulation is not recommended!

Q. **Based on all the information in the previous questions, about carrying a concealed gun, I would assume that there is no way anyone can do that without having a Pennsylvania License to Carry a Firearm, right?**

No, surprisingly enough, that *is not* right. Section 6106 (b) of the Uniform Firearms Act describes 11 classes of people who can carry a concealed firearm (handgun) without a license; and § 6106.1 explains that four of those eleven classes can also carry *loaded* rifles and shotguns in vehicles. Here are the most relevant exceptions in § 6106, to the requirement of having a License to carry a concealed handgun, each with an explanation of the restrictions placed on you by the exception. Exceptions for military and law enforcement personnel are *not* included here but *are* included in Part II, where the statutes are reprinted in their entirety.

§ 6106 (a.) No person shall carry a firearm in any vehicle or concealed on or about his person, except in his place of abode or fixed place of business . . . .

What this all means in English is that if you are in your house ("abode") you may carry your handgun concealed. It also means that you can carry it concealed while in your place of business that is "fixed." So, if you own a store, you can carry your gun (remember, the "gun" must be a handgun) while in the store; but if you are a traveling salesman, your "place of business" is probably your car. Your car may be fixed (repaired) but it is not in a "fixed" location (which is what the law refers to); and so you cannot carry a concealed gun on your person while in the car, or keep the gun in the car, without a License to Carry a Firearm.
[See 18 Pa. C.S. § 6106 (a) in this book.]

Here are the exceptions of § 6106 (b) (not in numerical sequence).

(8) Any person while carrying a firearm unloaded and in a secure wrapper from the place of purchase to his home or place of business, or to a place of repair or back to his home or place of business, or in moving from one place of abode or business to another or from his home to a vacation or recreational home or dwelling or back, or to recover stolen property under section 6111.1 (b) (4) (relating to Pennsylvania State Police) or to a location to which the person has been directed to surrender firearms under 23 Pa. C.S. § 6108 (relating to relief) or back upon return of the surrendered firearm.

You can carry the firearm (handgun) when it is **unloaded** and in a *secure wrapper.* Obviously, this will not make it feasible to use the handgun to protect yourself - because you will first have to unwrap it and load it. Carry the handgun, loaded and ready to use, and you would not be entitled to the exception. Get stopped by a law enforcement officer and you could lose the gun (have it confiscated) and lose your right to ever have a gun of any kind.

(4) *Any persons engaged in target shooting with rifle, pistol, or revolver, if such persons are at or are going to or from their places of assembly or target practice and if, while going to or from their places of assembly or target practice, the cartridges or shells are carried in a separate container and the rifle, pistol or revolver is unloaded.*

Again, you can carry a handgun - or in this case, rifles and shotguns also - but they must be unloaded and the cartridges should be in a separate container. (Remember, rifles and shotguns must **always** be carried unloaded, if in a vehicle; and neither are they permitted to be carried concealed.) Same comment about confiscation applies here as for (8), above.

(6) *Agents, messengers and other employees of common carriers, banks, or business firms, whose duties require them to protect moneys, valuables and other property in the discharge of such duties.*

These are people who can carry concealed handguns "in the discharge of such duties." That means that they can carry a concealed handgun while working, but certainly could not do so when **not** working. Thus, this exception is quite restrictive also. (These people are also in a class which is an exception to the prohibition against carrying a loaded rifle or shotgun in a vehicle.) Those people must also be certified under the Lethal Weapon Training Act, as described in this book (1974, P.L. 705, No. 235, commonly known as "Act 235").

*(9)   Persons licensed to hunt, take furbearers or fish in this Com-
monwealth, if such persons are actually hunting, taking furbearers or fishing or are going to the place where they desire
to hunt, take furbearers or fish or returning from such places.*

*(10) Persons training dogs, if such persons are actually training
dogs during the regular training season.*

Section 6106 specifies that these people can carry concealed
handguns while involved in the listed activities; and authoritative individuals in the State Police concur with this interpretation. However, other knowledgeable individuals have
indicated that there may be interpretations which permit carrying only exposed, and not concealed, handguns. Because
there is usually no reason to conceal a handgun in these
curcumstances it would be prudent to keep your handgun
exposed unless you also hold a License to Carry a Firearm.
Note also that persons claiming an exemption under (9) and
(10) are also required to obtain a **sportsman's firearm permit.** The permit is valid only when these people are hunting,
fishing, training dogs or going to, or returning from, the places
at which these activities are ocurring.

*(11) Any person while carrying a firearm in any vehicle which
person possesses a valid and lawfully issued license for that
firearm which has been issued under the laws of the United
States or any other state.*

This exception was added by Act 66. It acknowledges the
fact that the highways and streets of Pennsylvania might not
be the safest, and allows individuals who have a license from
any of our other forty-nine states, to carry a concealed handgun in their vehicle. Note however, that when the person
exits their vehicle, the handgun must **remain in the vehicle.**
A "memory lapse" resulting in the person carrying the gun
into a truck stop or restaurant could cause that person quite
a bit of trouble. It would be beneficial to all Americans if

similar legislation were passed in every state, allowing the highways to be a little safer for everyone.

As you can see, all these exceptions are quite restrictive. Thus, if you really need to be able to carry a concealed handgun with you, wherever you travel within Pennsylvania, the only way you will be able to do so is by meeting the requirements of the License to Carry a Firearm and obtaining that license.

Section 6122 is also of interest; that is the section that we referred to previously with regard to the "... *lawful demand of a law enforcement officer [to] produce the [License to Carry a Firearm] for inspection."* Well, § 6122 has two parts; the second part is: *"An individual carrying a firearm on or about his person or in a vehicle and claming an exception under section 6106 (b) (relating to firearms not to be carried without a license) shall, upon lawful demand of a law enforcement officer, produce satisfactory evidence of qualifications for exception."*

So, if you are going to carry a concealed firearm based on one of the exceptions listed in 6106 (b) or (c) [or 6110.1 (b) (2)], you'd better be prepared to prove to a law enforcement officer that you are entitled to the exception!
[See 18 Pa. C.S. § 6106 (a) through (d), § 6110.1 (b) (2), and § 6122 in this book.]

Q. Does my Pennsylvania License to Carry a Firearm entitle me to carry my concealed handgun in any other states?

A. Surprisingly, it does, although only in 5 states. Vermont permits all their adult citizens to carry concealed firearms without having a permit as long as they have "good character," as indicated by the lack of a criminal record, and "no malice in their hearts." Your license demonstrates that *you* have good character; and so you are allowed to carry your concealed handgun in Vermont. Michigan, Idaho, Wyoming and

Indiana also honor your license. (However, laws change so you should verify this before taking a gun to any of those states.) Although Act 17 provides for reciprocity at the option of the Attorney General of Pennsylvania *[see 18 Pa. C.S. § 6109 (k)]* Pennsylvania does not, at this time, accept any other state's license to carry concealed firearms except in their vehicles as described in a previous Q & A. Readers may care to note that the state of West Virginia has a standing offer of reciprocity with Pennsylvania. All that is needed for Pennsylvanians with a License to Carry a Firearm to be able to carry their guns in West Virginia is for the Attorney General of Pennsylvania to write a letter to West Virginia agreeing to the offer. So far that has not happened.

Q. **I keep hearing about the "assault weapon ban" on the television news. What exactly is an "assault weapon"? How do I know if I have one? What happens if I violate the law?**

A. By federal law, it has long been illegal for an individual to own, without a special tax stamp from the Treasury Department, any *fully automatic* weapon; that is, a gun that fires more than one time, after a single pull of the trigger. (Such guns are popularly known as "machine guns".) In September of 1994 a federal law was enacted which defined certain features of *semi-automatic guns* (guns that fire only one time, with each pull of the trigger) which made these guns "semi-automatic assault weapons." It is important to understand that these are legislative definitions, not definitions that any authoritative source, such as the book, *Jane's Infantry Weapons*, would offer.

According to the new law, it is unlawful to possess or transfer a semi-automatic assault weapon and violation of the law subjects the violator to a fine of up to $5000 and up to five years in prision. (And therefore, loss of your right to ever own a gun.) There is also a related statute which bans "large capacity ammunition feeding devices" - legal lingo for magazines ("clips") or anything else that holds more than 10 rounds of ammunition.

Fortunately for gun owners, this law does not apply to guns and devices which were *manufactured* before the date of enactment of the law, September 13, 1994. You may keep and use any semi-automatic assault weapon or ammunition feeding device you now own, or sell it or do anything lawful with it, as long as it was manufactured before the above date.

As expected, the semi-automatic assault weapon ban does not apply to the usual list of exceptions - certain law enforcement officers, members of the Armed Forces, etc. It *does* apply to most everyone else; and if you get caught with a semi-automatic assault weapon you are subject to the penalties described, *even if you didn't know the weapon was a semi-automatic assault weapon.*

How do you know if a semi-automatic assault weapon you own or that someone wants to sell or give to you, is a prohibited semi-automatic assault weapon? Well, all semi-automatic assault weapons that were made after September 13, 1994 are required to have a serial number that shows the date they were manufactured and be marked "RESTRICTED LAW ENFORCEMENT/GOVERNMENT USE ONLY" or "FOR EXPORT ONLY." But, if you inadvertently possess or transfer a semi-automatic assault weapon made after that date, that for some reason, is not marked with the date, you are still guilty of the violation. The BATF advises dealers who receive semi-automatic assault weapons without markings to indicate date of manufacture, to obtain an invoice, bill of sale or other documentation indicating that weapon was lawfully possessed before September 13, 1994. You would be advised to obtain the same information in such a situation.

RIFLES

Any semi-automatic rifle that can accept a detachable magazine ("clip") and has at least two of the features listed below, is an assault weapon.

- ☐ A folding or telescoping stock
- ☐ A pistol grip that protrudes conspicuously beneath the action of the gun
- ☐ A bayonet mount
- ☐ A flash suppressor or threaded barrel designed to accommodate a flash suppressor
- ☐ A grenade launcher

PISTOLS

Any semi-automatic pistol that can accept a detachable magazine ("clip") and that has at least two of the features listed below is an assault weapon.

- ☐ An ammunition magazine that attaches to the pistol outside of the pistol grip
- ☐ A threaded barrel capable of accepting a barrel extender, flash suppressor, forward handgrip or silencer
- ☐ A manufactured weight of 50 ounces or more when the pistol is unloaded
- ☐ A shroud that is attached to the barrel (or partially or completely encircles it) and that permits the shooter to hold the gun with the nontrigger hand without being burned
- ☐ A semi-automatic version of an automatic gun

SHOTGUNS

Any semi-automatic shotgun that has at least two of the features listed below is considered an assault weapon.

- ☐ A folding or telescoping stock
- ☐ A pistol grip that protrudes conspicuously beneath the action of the gun
- ☐ A fixed magazine capacity in excess of five rounds
- ☐ An ability to accept a detachable magazine

EXCEPTIONS TO THE FEDERAL BAN ON ASSAULT WEAPONS

- [ ] Guns manufactured on or before the date the federal crime bill was enacted, September 13, 1994
- [ ] Any gun listed in Title 22 of the United States Code, Section 922, Appendix A, as such guns were manufactured on or before October 1, 1993 (which predates the September 13, 1994 enactment date). Also replicas and duplicates of these guns. (These guns are mostly hunting and historic guns and are not typical assault weapons.)
- [ ] Guns that are manually operated by bolt, pump, lever or slide action
- [ ] Semi-automatic rifles that cannot accept detachable magazines that hold more than five rounds of ammunition
- [ ] Semi-automatic shotguns that cannot hold more than five rounds of ammunition in a fixed or detachable magazine
- [ ] Guns that are considered antique firearms under federal law
- [ ] Guns that have been modified so that they can never fire (guns that are "rendered permanently inoperable")

LARGE CAPACITY AMMUNITION FEEDING DEVICES

Any magazine, belt, drum, feed strip or other device that can hold, or be readily restored or converted to hold, more than ten rounds of ammunition is a large capacity ammunition feeding device; and all such devices manufactured after the date the federal crime bill was enacted, September 13, 1994, are unlawful to possess or transfer.

The penalties for violating this law are the same as for violating the law on assault weapons. And, as with assault weapons, inadvertent violation, because the required date is not on the devices, is still a violation subject to the full penalty.

The only exception to the law is for attached tubular magazines or other tubular devices that hold *only .22 caliber rimfire ammunition.*

Q. I noticed comments in previous Q & A's indicating that being caught with an illegal knife could prevent me from owning a gun. What makes a knife "illegal"?

A. In some states, statutes list a whole slew of characteristics that could make a knife illegal - the way it opens, the length, whether both edges are sharpened, and so on. But in Pennsylvania the law is extremely vague. The only knives - or "cutting instruments" as they are described in the statute - that are specified as illegal are those, *"the blade of which is exposed in an automatic way by switch, push-button, spring mechanism, or otherwise, or other implement for the infliction of serious bodily injury which serves no common lawful purpose."*

So does that mean you can walk down the street with an eight inch dagger concealed under your jacket? Hardly. The general belief is that the law was left deliberately vague so that law enforcement officers, district attorneys and the courts would be free to let the circumstances under which the knife were being carried dictate whether the knife would be considered illegal - that is, whether it was a "prohibited offensive weapon."

For example, go out hunting with your buddies, and have a knife with a seven inch, double edged blade, swinging from your side ... and "the law" probably wouldn't even take notice of it. Carry that same knife, concealed or in the open, on a city street, and you will likely get a lot of attention from the law.

Similarly, a Fortune 500 executive with a belt buckle knife worn as an anti-kidnapping device would likely not be bothered. Neither would a worker for a food distributor who carries a knife with a five inch blade in a sheath on his side for use in opening up crates of tomatoes and asparagus. But if that same worker were found by police in a bar, with that same knife in a sheath under

his shirt, he would very possibly end up being late . . . very late
. . . to work the next morning.

A good rule of thumb for most people is that a single edged knife
with a blade of 3" or less is usually regarded with a lot *less*
suspicion than a double edged knife or a single edged knife with
a longer blade. And lock back folding knives can be regarded
with *more* suspicion than their non-lock back cousins. In the
author's experience, multifunction ("Swiss Army") knives are
virtually "invisible." The author has carried his multifunction
knife, dangling outside his trouser pocket, onto dozens of airplanes over the last 10 years and has not been questioned a single
time. *(Perhaps being accompanied by a wife and four children
had something to do with that.)*

Not sure what to do? Just remember, if you're carrying a knife
to use as a weapon, whether defensively or otherwise, the police
are likely to come to the same conclusion - and place you under
arrest. If convicted, and if your sentence could have been more
than one year in prison, even if the sentence is suspended
and/or you are put on probation and serve no time at all, you
become a member of one of the classes of people that is prohibited from ever possessing, receiving, shipping or transporting firearms (including rifles and shotguns) or ammunition.
[See 18 Pa. C.S. § 908 in this book.]

**Q. OK, if I don't want to carry a gun for self-defense, and I can't
carry a knife, and my schedule is too full to take up kung fu
. . . what can I carry to protect myself?**

A. How about a chemical defense spray? "Mace®" was the original
chemical defense spray. Being the first of its kind it became so
well known that the very word "Mace®" became a generic name
for any kind of chemical defense spray, in the same way that
"Kleenex®" became a household generic word for facial tissue.
Advances in technology have come up with more effective chemical sprays and "pepper spray" is now considered to be the best
such self-defense product to carry.

One very beneficial aspect of chemical defense sprays, such as pepper spray, is that Pennsylvania has no statutes regulating it. State legislators have apparently taken the position that the "bad guys" tend to use more prosaic methods - weapons, strength, general nastiness - and bad breath; so the "good guys" should have the opportunity to defend themselves by using chemical defense sprays.

There are two important factors to be aware of concerning chemical sprays. First, although Pennsylvania does not regulate their use, other states do. Be sure to check chemical defense spray laws in states you are traveling to, if you intend to carry a chemical defense spray with you. There are some states in which possession or use of a chemical defense spray is treated with almost the same severity as carrying an unlicensed handgun. It sometimes makes you wonder whose side the legislators are on . . . or if they were out playing golf when brains were handed out.

Second, chemical defense sprays - and especially, pepper spray - vary widely in their effectiveness. There are many "rip-off artists" who offer a significantly diluted (and significantly less effective) product - either at a low price, so you think you got a bargain, or at a high price because they figure you won't know the difference.

The *really good* pepper sprays can be quite incapacitating; the *not very good* pepper sprays can be . . . well, one individual told this author that he takes his not-so-good pepper spray to Chinese restaurants where he uses it to spice up some of the blander dishes.

It is extremely important to get the best spray. You may only have to use your pepper spray once in your life. . . but when you do, you want to remember that it worked and saved you . . . not that it didn't work but you saved three bucks by buying the cheaper version.

Q. In some of the answers presented previously, comments are made about violations of specific laws being summary offenses or third degree misdemeanors or .... How do these comments relate to a specific period of time I could be sent to jail if I violate those laws.

A. As explained in the Pennsylvania Crimes Code, an offense for which a sentence of death or imprisonment is authorized, constitutes a crime. Each crime is assigned a "class" (first degree murder, third degree felony, etc.); and each class has associated with it, a maximum sentence that can be imposed. For example, if you commit a crime which is classified as a second degree felony, you can be sentenced to a term of imprisonment up to 10 years. The classes of offenses and the maximum terms of imprisonment associated with them will be found in Part II, as listed below.
[See 18 Pa. C.S. § 106 and also 42 Pa. C.S. § 9712, § 9754, § 9763 in this book.]

Q. Throughout this book I have read time and again of technicalities and absurd applications of the law, which could result in my paying big fines, losing my guns or even being imprisoned. I understand why some people say, "The law is an ass." Is there any defense against ridiculous laws or the misapplication of good laws by overzealous or gun-hating prosecutors and judges?

A. Actually there is. Years ago, juries had the right to judge, not only the guilt or innocence of the defendant, but also the reasonableness of the law under which the defendant was being charged. The juries had the right to find a defendant, "not guilty," if they felt the law was unjustly applied or if they felt the law itself was bad. The juries were "fully informed" of their right do this by the judges and defense attorneys. (One of the early results of "fully informed juries" was the Revolutionary War!)

Sometime around the turn of the 20th century, the tide turned; and, in order to retain complete control over the decisions in their courtrooms (despite the fact that they were *supposed to be* impartial) judges stopped telling juries of their rights. And some judges went so far as to *refuse to allow* defendants or defense attorneys to tell the juries of their rights. All this has happened despite the fact that the U.S. Supreme Court has stated, in several instances, that juries have the right to be fully informed that they may judge the law as well as the defendant.

An organization named FIJA - the Fully Informed Jury Association - was established some years ago. Their goal is to pass legislation in every state requiring juries to be fully informed of their rights to judge both the law and the defendant. A fully informed jury could, some day, help keep *YOU* out of prison!

To learn more about FIJA and fully informed juries, please refer to the offer of updated information on the gun laws, plus important reports, at the very back of this book.

This concludes *Part I: Questions and Answers About Owning and Using Guns in Pennsylvania.*

We encourage readers to write to us and tell us about other situations for which Q & A's would be helpful. We will certainly consider those suggestions for future revisions and updates of this book.

Anyone who submits a suggestion which is incorporated into future editions will be mailed three complimentary copies of the first edition that includes their suggestion.

PART II
PENNSYLVANIA LAWS RELATING TO GUNS

In Pennsylvania law, large groupings of statutes (laws) concerning related subjects are designated *Titles* or *Public Laws*. The basic unit of information within each large grouping, which usually concerns just a single topic is a "section." Part II consists of most of the sections that relate to guns, excerpted from a number of Titles and Public Laws, and includes all the sections cited in Part I. For brevity, *only* the section number, not the Title or Public Law from which it came, is listed in the index below; thus there will be some duplication of section numbers. (For example, every Title and Public Law starts out with section 1.) For that reason, the official descriptions of the content of each section are listed next to each section number. *[Bracketed descriptions are additions by the author.]* At the end of each section is a complete citation including its source Title or Public Law and any other necessary information.

Although we have tried to group sections containing similar subject matter together, without regard to the statutes from which they were excerpted, there may be sections on related matters, which appear elsewhere in Part II or which are not printed in this book at all.

ACTS 17 & 66 AND RELATED GUN LAWS

EMERGENCY MANAGEMENT

GAME AND WILDLIFE - SPORTING USE OF GUNS

MUNICIPAL REGULATION OF FIREARMS

LETHAL WEAPONS TRAINING ACT

OTHER TRAINING AND EDUCAITON

DOMESTIC RELATIONS

CRIMES AND OFFENSES GENERALLY

SENTENCING

ACTS 17 & 66 AND RELATED GUN LAWS

The "new Pennsylvania Gun Law" was originally introduced as Senate Bill Number 6, and Special House Bill Number 110, and having been signed into law, is now known as Act 17. The bill was signed into law on June 13, 1995 and it took effect 120 days after that date, on October 11, 1995. Until that time, the "old" laws were in effect. The amendments to Act 17 were part of Senate Bill Number 282, and having been signed into law, are now part of Act 66. The bill was signed into law on November 22, 1995 and took effect on that date (some parts) and at later dates (other parts), as described in section 13 of Senate Bill Number 282, reproduced below.

At the end of each section is a section citation which specifies the title or public law from which the section was excerpted. If the section was unchanged by Acts 17 and/or 66, then only the source title or public law is listed in the citation. If the section was added or altered by Act 17 then "Act 17" is printed at the end of the section citation. If the section was added or altered by Act 66, then "Act 66" and the number of days after the November 22, 1995 signing or the date that the change becomes effective, may be printed at the end of the section citation.

ACT 17 INTRODUCTION & PREAMBLE

AMENDING TITLES 18 (CRIMES AND OFFENSES) AND 42 (JUDICIARY AND JUDICIAL PROCEDURE) OF THE PENNSYLVANIA CONSOLIDATED STATUTES, FURTHER PROVIDING FOR THE POSSESSION OF FIREARMS; ESTABLISHING A SELECTED STATEWIDE JUVENILE OFFENDER REGISTRY; AND MAKING AN APPROPRIATION.
[Act 17]

The General Assembly hereby declares that the purpose of this act is to provide support to law enforcement in the area of crime prevention and control, that it is not the purpose of this act to place any undue or unnecessary restrictions or burdens on law-abiding citizens with respect to the acquisition, possession, transfer, transportation or use of firearms, rifles or shotguns for personal protection, hunting, target shooting, employment or any other lawful activity, and that this act is not intended to discourage or restrict the private ownership and use of firearms by law-abiding citizens for lawful purposes, or to provide for the imposition by rules or regulations of any procedures or requirements other than those necessary to implement

and effectuate the provisions of this act. The General Assembly hereby recognizes and declares its support of the fundamental constitutional right of Commonwealth citizens to bear arms in defense of themselves and this Commonwealth.
[Act 17]

[Author's Note: The above so-called "reaffirmation" of the constitutional right of Pennsylvania citizens to own and use guns is part of the preamble to Act 17 and is not a part of the statute itself. When Act 17 is printed in the statute books this preamble will not appear with the firearms laws, but rather in the Appendix to Title 18, which deals with crimes and offenses of all types. Thus, this "reaffirmation" will be one short paragraph at the end of some 160 pages of text. If an attorney were to cite the preamble as a defense, a jurist (judge) would likely rule that the preamble is merely a comment, not part of the law itself, and would not give it much weight.]

———— SECTION 12 of H.B. No. 110 ————

(a) The sum of $1,200,000 or as much thereof as may be necessary, is hereby appropriated to the Pennsylvania State Police for the fiscal year July 1, 1995, to June 30, 1996, for the administration of 18 Pa. C.S. Ch. 61 (relating to firearms and other dangerous articles).

(b) The appropriation in subsection (a) shall not lapse at the end of the fiscal year but shall continue for two fiscal years.
[Act 17]

ACT 66 INTRODUCTION

AMENDING TITLE 18 (CRIMES AND OFFENSES) OF THE PENNSYLVANIA CONSOLIDATED STATUTES, DEFINING "POLICE OFFICER"; DEFINING "LAW ENFORCEMENT OFFICER" AND "LOADED" FOR PURPOSES OF THE UNIFORM FIREARMS ACT OF 1995; FURTHER PROVIDING FOR CERTAIN PROHIBITED CRIMINAL CONDUCT, FOR ADMINISTRATION, FOR FEES AND FOR NOTIFICATION; . . . AND MAKING REPEALS.
[Act 66]

———— SECTION 13 of S.B. No. 282 ————

This act shall take effect as follows:

    * * *

    (2) The addition of 18 Pa. C.S. § 6111 (b) (1.1) shall take effect January 1, 1997.

    (3) The addition of 18 Pa. C.S. § 6126 shall take effect July 1, 1996.

(4) The amendment or addition of 18 Pa. C.S. § 6315 . . . shall take effect in 60 days.

* * *

(6) The remainder of this act shall take effect immediately.

[Act 66]

―――――――――― **SECTION 6101** ――――――――――
Short Title of Subchapter

This subchapter shall be known and may be cited as the Pennsylvania Uniform Firearms Act of 1995.

[18 Pa. C.S. § 6101; Act 17]

[Author's Note: Section 6101 above uses the words, *"this subchapter."* The meaning of these words is as follows. *Title 18* is the group of Pennsylvania statutes (laws) that concerns "Crimes and Offenses," and, as such, is officially designated the "Crimes Code." Title 18 treats numerous types of crimes, and these are separated into chapters. *Chapter 61* deals with *"Firearms and Other Dangerous Articles."* Within Chapter 61 are several subchapters including subchapter A, the Pennsylvania Uniform Firearms Act of 1995. Within subchapter A are many sections and subsections; and those which deal with guns are reproduced here.

Thus § 6101 above has explained that much (but not all) of what follows is part of subchapter A, "The Uniform Firearms Act of 1995." (Prior to the passage of Act 17, that subchapter was named, simply, the "Pennsylvania Uniform Firearms Act," with no designation of year.) Our presentation, here in Part II, includes both old and new statutes relating to guns; that is, those in both the old and new Uniform Firearms Acts, as well as those not in the Uniform Firearms Act but found elsewhere in Pennsylvania's legal code.]

―――――――――― **SECTION 6102** ――――――――――
Definitions

Subject to additional definitions contained in subsequent provisions of this subchapter which are applicable to specific provisions of this subchapter, the following words and phrases, when used in this subchapter shall have, unless the context clearly indicates otherwise, the meanings given to them in this section:

"Commissioner." The commissioner of the Pennsylvania State Police.

"Conviction." A conviction, a finding of guilty or the entering of a plea of guiltyor nolo contendere, whether or not judgment of sentence has been imposed, as determined by the law of the jurisdiction in which the prosecution was held. The term does not include a conviction which has been expunged or overturned or for which an individual has been pardoned unless the pardon expressly provides that the individual may not possess or transport firearms.

"County Treasurer." The county treasurer or, in home rule or optional plan counties, the person whose duties encompass those of a county treasurer.

"Crime punishable by imprisonment exceeding one year." The term does not include any of the following:

(1) Federal or state offenses pertaining to antitrust, unfair trade practices, restraints on trade or regulation of business.
(2) State offenses classified as misdemeanors and punishable by a term of imprisonment not to exceed two years.

"Firearm." Any pistol or revolver with a barrel length less than 15 inches, any shotgun with a barrel length less than 18 inches or any rifle with a barrel length less than 16 inches, or any pistol, revolver, rifle or shotgun with an overall length of less than 26 inches. The barrel length of a firearm shall be determined by measuring from the muzzle of the barrel to the face of the closed action, bolt or cylinder, whichever is applicable.

"Fund." The Firearm Ownership Fund established in section 6111.3 (relating to Firearm Ownership Fund).

[Author's Note: Act 17 changed the name of this fund *from* Firearm Ownership Fund *to* Firearm Instant Records Check Fund.]

"Law enforcement officer." Any person employed by any police department or organization of the Commonwealth or political subdivision thereof who is empowered to effect an arrest with or without warrant and who is authorized to carry a firearm in the performance of that person's duties.

"Loaded." A firearm is loaded if the firing chamber, the nondetachable magazine, or in the case of a revolver, any of the chambers of the cylinder, contain ammunition capable of being fired. In the case of a firearm which utilizes a detachable magazine, the term shall mean a magazine suitable for use in said firearm which magazine contains such ammunition and has been inserted in the firearm or is in the same container or, where the container has multiple compartments, the same compartment thereof as the firearm.

"Sheriff."

    (1) Except as provided in paragraph (2), the sheriff of the county.

    (2) In a city of the first class, the chief or head of the police department.
[18 Pa. C.S. § 6102; Act 17; Act 66, eff. imm.]

SECTION 6103
Crimes Committed With Firearms

If any person commits or attempts to commit a crime enumerated in section 6105 (relating to persons not to possess, use, manufacture, control, sell or transfer firearms) when armed with a firearm contrary to the provisions of this subchapter, that person may, in addition to the punishment provided for the crime, also be punished as provided by this subchapter.
[18 Pa. C.S. § 6103; Act 17]

SECTION 6104
Evidence of Intent

In the trial of a person for committing or attempting to commit a crime enumerated in section 6105 (relating to persons not to possess, use, manufacture, control, sell or transfer firearms), the fact that that person was armed with a firearm, used or attempted to be used, and had no license to carry the same, shall be evidence of that person's intention to commit the offense.
[18 Pa. C.S. § 6104; Act 17]

SECTION 6105
Persons Not to Possess, Use, Manufacture, Control, Sell or Transfer Firearms.

(a) Offense defined.

    (1) A person who has been convicted of an offense enumerated in subsection (b), within or without this Commonwealth, regardless of the length of sentence or whose conduct meets the criteria in subsection (c) shall not possess, use, control, sell, transfer or manufacture or obtain a license to possess, use, control, sell, transfer or manufacture a firearm in this Commonwealth.

    A person who is prohibited from possessing, using, controlling, selling, transferring or manufacturing a firearm under paragraph (1) or subsection (b) or (c) shall have a reasonable period of time not to exceed 60 days from the date of the imposition of the disability under this subsection in which to sell or transfer that person's firearms to another eligible person who is not a member of the prohibited person's household.

82

(b) Enumerated offenses. The following offenses shall apply to subsection (a):

Section 908 (relating to prohibited offensive weapons).

Section 911 (relating to corrupt organizations).

Section 912 (relating to possession of weapon on school property).

Section 2502 (relating to murder).

Section 2503 (relating to voluntary manslaughter).

Section 2504 (relating to involuntary manslaughter) if the offense is based on the reckless use of a firearm.

Section 2702 (relating to aggravated assault).

Section 2703 (relating to assault by prisoner).

Section 2704 (relating to assault by life prisoner).

Section 2709 (relating to harassment and stalking) if the offense relates to stalking.

Section 2901 (relating to kidnapping).

Section 2902 (relating to unlawful restraint).

Section 2910 (relating to luring a child into a motor vehicle).

Section 3121 (relating to rape).

Section 3123 (relating to involuntary deviate sexual intercourse).

Section 3125 (relating to aggravated indecent assault).

Section 3301 (relating to arson and related offensees).

Section 3302 (relating to causing or risking catastrophe).

Section 3502 (relating to burglary).

Section 3503 (relating to criminal trespass) if the offense is graded a felony of the second degree or higher.

Section 3701 (relating to robbery).

Section 3702 (relating to robbery of motor vehicle).

Section 3921 (relating to theft by unlawful taking or disposition) upon conviction of the second felony offense.

Section 3923 (relating to theft by extortion) when the offense is accompanied by threats of violence.

Section 3925 (relating to receiving stolen property) upon conviction of the second felony offense.

Section 4912 (relating to impersonating a public servant) if the person is impersonating a law enforcement officer.

Section 4952 (relating to intimidation of witnesses or victims).

Section 4953 (relating to retaliation against witness or victim).

Section 5121 (relating to escape).

Section 5122 (relating to weapons or implements for escape).

Section 5501 (3) (relating to riot).

Section 5515 (relating to prohibiting of paramilitary training).

Section 6110.1 (relating to possession of firearm by minor).

Section 6301 (relating to corruption of minors).

Section 6302 (relating to sale or lease of weapons and explosives).

Any offense equivalent to any of the above-enumerated offenses under the prior laws of this Commonwealth or any offense equivalent to any of the above enumerated offenses under the statutes of any other state or of the United States.

(c) **Other persons.** In addition to any person who has been convicted of any offense listed under subsection (b), the following persons shall be subject to the prohibition of subsection (a):

(1) A person who is a fugitive from justice.

(2) A person who has been convicted of an offense under the act of April 14, 1972 (P.L. 233, No. 64), known as the Controlled Substance, Drug, Device and Cosmetic Act that may be punishable by a term of imprisonment exceeding two years.

(3) A person who has been convicted of driving under the influence of alcohol or controlled substance as provided in 75 Pa. C.S. § 3731 (relating to driving under influence of alcohol or controlled substance) on three or more separate occasions within a five-year period. For the purposes of this paragraph only, the prohibition of subsection (a) shall only apply to transfers or purchases of firearms after the third conviction.

(4) A person who has been adjudicated as an incompetent or who has been involuntarily committed to a mental institution for inpatient care and treatment under section 302, 303 or 304 of the provisions of the act of July 9, 1976 (P.L. 817, No. 143), known as the Mental Health Procedures Act.

(5) A person who, being an alien, is illegally or unlawfully in the United States.

(6) A person who is the subject of an active protection from abuse order issued pursuant to 23 Pa. C.S. § 6108 (relating to relief) which order provided for the confiscation of firearms during the period of time the order is in effect. This prohibition shall terminate upon the expiration or vacation of an active protection from abuse order or portion there of relating to the confiscation of firearms.

(7) A person who was adjudicated delinquent by a court pursuant to 42 Pa. C.S. § 6341 (relating to adjudication) or under any equivalent federal statute or statute of any other state as a result of conduct which if committed by an adult would constitute an offense under sections 2502, 2503, 2702, 2703 (relating to assault by prisoner), 2704, 2901, 3121, 3123, 3301, 3502, 3701 and 3923.

(8) A person who was adjudicated delinquent by a court pursuant to 42 Pa. C.S. § 6341 or under any equivalent federal statute or statute of any other state as a result of conduct which if committed by an adult would constitute an offense enumerated in

subsection (b) with the exception of those crimes set forth in paragraph (7). This prohibition shall terminate 15 years after the last applicable delinquent adjudication or upon the person reaching the age of 30, whichever is earlier.

(d) Exemption. A person who has been convicted of a crime specified in subsection (a) or (b) or a person whose conduct meets the criteria in subsection (c) (1), (2), (5) or (7) may make application to the Court of Common Pleas of the county where the principal residence of the applicant is situated for relief from the disability imposed by this section upon the possession, transfer or control of a firearm. The court shall grant such relief if it determines that any of the following apply:

(1) The conviction has been vacated under circumstances where all appeals have been exhausted or where the right to appeal has expired.

(2) The conviction has been the subject of a full pardon by the governor.

(3) Each of the following conditions is met:

(i) The Secretary of the Treasury of the United States has relieved the applicant of an applicable disability imposed by federal law upon the possession, ownership or control of a firearm as a result of the applicant's prior conviction, except that the court may waive this condition if the court determines that the Congress of the United States has not appropriated sufficient funds to enable the Secretary of the Treasury to grant relief to applicants eligible for the relief.

(ii) A period of ten years, not including any time spent in incarceration, has elapsed since the most recent conviction of the applicant of a crime enumerated in subsection (b) or a felony violation of the Controlled Substance, Drug, Device and Cosmetic Act.

Proceedings.

(1) If a person convicted of an offense under subsection (a), (b) or (c) (1), (2), (5) or (7) makes application to the court, a hearing shall be held in open court to determine whether the requirements of this section have been met. The commissioner and the District Attorney of the county where the application is filed and any victim or survivor of a victim of the offense upon which the disability is based may be parties to the proceeding.

(2) Upon application to the Court of Common Pleas pursuant to paragraph (1) by an applicant who is subject to the prohibition under subsection (c) (3), the court shall grant such relief if a period of ten years, not including any time spent in incarceration, has passed since the applicant's most recent conviction under subsection (c) (3).

(f) Other exemptions and proceedings.

(1) Upon application to the Court of Common Pleas under this subsection by an applicant subject to the prohibitions under subsection (c) (4), the court may grant such relief as it deems appropriate if the court determines that the applicant may possess a firearm without risk to the applicant or any other person.

(2) If application is made under this subsection for relief from the disability imposed under subsection (c) (6), notice of such application shall be given to the person who had petitioned for the protection from abuse order and such person shall be a party to the proceedings. Notice of any court order or amendment to a court order restoring firearms possession or control shall be given to the person who had petitioned for the protection from abuse order.

(3) All hearings conducted under this subsection shall be closed.

(g) Other restrictions. Nothing in this section shall exempt a person from a disability in relation to the possession or control of a firearm which is imposed as a condition of probation or parole or which is imposed pursuant to the provision of any law other than this section.

(h) License prohibition. Any person who is prohibited from possessing, using, controlling, selling, purchasing, transferring or manufacturing any firearm under this section shall not be eligible for or permitted to obtain a license to carry a firearm under section 6109 (relating to licenses).

(i) Firearm. As used in this section only, the term "firearm" shall include any weapons which are designed to or may readily be converted to expel any projectile by the action of an explosive or the frame or receiver of any such weapon. *[18 Pa. C.S. § 6105; Act 17; Act 66, eff. imm.]*

SECTION 6123
Waiver of Disability or Pardons

A waiver of disability from Federal authorities as provided for in 18 U.S.C. § 925 (relating to exceptions; relief from disabilities), a full pardon from the Governor or an overturning of a conviction shall remove any corresponding disability under this subchapter except the disability under section 6105 (relating to persons not to possess, use, manufacture, control, sell or transfer firearms).

[18 Pa. C.S. § 6123; Act 66, eff. imm.]

SECTION 6106
Firearms Not To Be Carried Without A License

(a) **Offense defined.** Any person who carries a firearm in any vehicle or any person who carries a firearm concealed on or about his person, except in his place of abode or fixed place of business, without a valid and lawfully issued license under this chapter commits a felony of the third degree.

(b) **Exceptions.** The provisions of subsection (a) shall not apply to:

(1) Constables, sheriffs, prison or jail wardens, or their deputies, policemen of this Commonwealth or its political subdivisions, or other law-enforcement officers.

(2) Members of the army, navy or marine corps of the United States or of the National Guard or organized reserves when on duty.

(3) The regularly enrolled members of any organization duly organized to purchase or receive such weapons from the United States or from this Commonwealth.

(4) Any persons engaged in target shooting with rifle, pistol, or revolver, if such persons are at or are going to or from their places of assembly or target practice and if, while going to or from their places of assembly or target practice, the cartridges or shells are carried in a separate container and the rifle, pistol or revolver is unloaded.

(5) Officers or employees of the United States duly authorized to carry a concealed firearm.

(6) Agents, messengers and other employees of common carriers, banks, or business firms, whose duties require them to protect moneys, valuables and other property in the discharge of such duties.

(7) Any person engaged in the business of manufacturing, repairing, or dealing in firearms, or the agent or representative of any such person, having in his possession, using or carrying a firearm in the usual or ordinary course of such business.

(8) Any person while carrying a firearm unloaded and in a secure wrapper from the place of purchase to his home or place of business, or to a place of repair or back to his home or place of business, or in moving from one place of abode or business to another or from his home to a vacation or recreational home or dwelling or back, or to recover stolen property under section 6111.1 (b) (4) (relating to Pennsylvania State Police) or to a location to

which the person has been directed to surrender firearms under 23 Pa. C.S. § 6108 (relating to relief) or back upon return of the surrendered firearm.

(9) Persons licensed to hunt, take furbearers or fish in this Common wealth, if such persons are actually hunting, taking furbearers or fishing or are going to the places where they desire to hunt, take furbearers or fish or returning from such places.

(10) Persons training dogs, if such persons are actually training dogs during the regular training season.

(11) Any person while carrying a firearm in any vehicle which person possesses a valid and lawfully issued license for that firearm which has been issued under the laws of the United States or any other state.

(c) Sportsman's firearm permit.

(1) Before any exception shall be granted under paragraph (b) (9) or (10) of this section to any person 18 years of age or older licensed to hunt, trap or fish or who has been issued a permit relating to hunting dogs, such person shall, at the time of securing his hunting, furtaking or fishing license or any time after such license has been issued, secure a sportsman's firearm permit from the county treasurer. The sportsman's firearm permit shall be issued immediately and be valid throughout this Commonwealth for a period of five years from the date of issue for any legal firearm, when carried in conjunction with a valid hunting, furtaking or fishing license or permit relating to hunting dogs. The sportsman's firearm permit shall be in triplicate on a form to be furnished by the Pennsylvania State Police. The original permit shall be delivered to the person, and the first copy thereof, within seven days, shall be forwarded to the Commissioner of the Pennsylvania State Police by the county treasurer. The second copy shall be retained by the county treasurer for a period of two years from the date of expiration. The county treasurer shall be entitled to collect a fee of not more than $6 for each such permit issued, which shall include the cost of any official form. The Pennsylvania state Police may recover from the county treasurer the cost of any such form, but may not charge more than $1 for each official permit form furnished to the county treasurer.

(2) Any person who sells or attempts to sell a sportsman's firearm permit for a fee in excess of that amount fixed under this subsection commits a summary offense.

(d) Revocation of registration. Any registration of a firearm under subsection (c) of this section may be revoked by the county treasurer who issued

it, upon written notice to the holder thereof.
[18 Pa. C.S. § 6106; Act 66, eff. imm.]

SECTION 6106.1

Carrying Loaded Weapons Other Than Firearms

(a) Genreal rule. Except as provided in 34 Pa. C.S. (relating to game), no person shall carry a loaded pistol, revolver, shotgun or rifle, other than a firearm as defined in section 6102 (relating to definitions), in any vehicle. The provisions of this section shall not apply to persons excepted from the requirement of a License to Carry Firearms under section 6106 (b) (1), (2), (5) or (6) (relating to firearms not to be carried without a license) nor shall the provisions of this section be construed to permit persons to carry firearms in a vehicle where such conduct is prohibited by section 6106.

(b) Penalty. A person who violates the provisions of this section commits a summary offense.

[18 Pa. C.S. § 6106.1; Act 17]

SECTION 6107

Prohibited Conduct During Emergency

No person shall carry a firearm, rifle or shotgun upon the public streets or upon any public property during an emergency proclaimed by a state or municipal governmental executive unless that person is:

(1) actively engaged in a defense of that person's life or property from peril or threat.

(2) licensed to carry firearms under section 6109 (relating to licenses) or is exempt from licensing under section 6106 (b) (relating to firearms not to be carried without a license).

[18 Pa. C.S. § 6107; Act 17]

SECTION 6108

Carrying Firearms on Public Streets or Public Property in Philadelphia

No person shall carry a firearm, rifle or shotgun at any time upon the public streets or upon any public property in a city of the first class unless:

(1) such person is licensed to carry a firearm; or

(2) such person is exempt from licensing under section 6106 (b) of this title (relating to firearms not to be carried without a license).

[18 Pa. C.S. § 6108]

SECTION 6109

Licenses

(a) Purpose of License. A license to carry a firearm shall be for the purpose of carrying a firearm concealed on or about one's person or in a vehicle within this Commonwealth. Any person who carries a firearm concealed on or about his person or in a vehicle within this Commonwealth without a valid and lawfully issued license under this section commits a felony of the third degree.

(b) **Place of application.** An individual who is 21 years of age or older may apply to a sheriff for a license to carry a firearm concealed on or about his person or in a vehicle within this Commonwealth. If the applicant is a resident of this Commonwealth, he shall make application with the sheriff of the county in which he resides or, if a resident of a city of the first class, with the chief of police of that city.

(c) **Form of application and content.** The application for a license to carry a firearm shall be uniform throughout this Commonwealth and shall be on a form prescribed by the Pennsylvania State Police. The form may contain provisions, not exceeding one page, to assure compliance with this section. Issuing authorities shall use only the application form prescribed by the Pennsylvania State Police. One of the following reasons for obtaining a firearm license shall be set forth in the application: self-defense, employment, hunting and fishing, target shooting, gun collecting or another proper reason. The application form shall be dated and signed by the applicant and shall contain the following statement:

> I have never been convicted of a crime of violence in the Commonwealth of Pennsylvania or elsewhere. I am of sound mind and have never been committed to a mental institution. I hereby certify that the statements contained herein are true and correct to the best of my knowledge and belief. I understand that, if I knowingly make any false statements herein, I am subject to penalties prescribed by law. I authorize the sheriff, or his designee, or, in the case of first class cities, the chief or head of the police department, or his designee, to inspect only those records or documents relevant to information required for this application.

(d) **Sheriff to conduct investigation.** The sheriff to whom the application is made shall investigate the applicant's record of criminal convictions, shall investigate whether or not the applicant is under indictment for or has ever been convicted of a crime punishable by imprisonment exceeding one year, shall investigate whether the applicant's character and reputation are such that the applicant will not be likely to act in a manner dangerous to public safety and shall investigate whether the applicant would be precluded from receiving a license under subsection (e) (1) or section 6105 (h) (relating to persons not to possess, use, manufacture, control, sell or transfer firearms) and shall conduct a criminal background, juvenile delinquency or mental health check following the procedures set forth in section 6111 (relating to firearm ownership).

(e) Issuance of license.

(1) A license to carry a firearm shall be for the purpose of carrying a firearm concealed on or about one's person or in a vehicle and shall be issued if, after an investigation not to exceed 45 days, it appears that the applicant is an individual concerning whom no good cause exists to deny the license. A license shall not be issued to any of the following:

(i) An individual whose character and reputation is such that the individual would be likely to act in a manner dangerous to public safety.

(ii) An individual who has been convicted of an offense under the act of April 14, 1972 (P.L. 233, No. 64), known as the Controlled Substance, Drug, Device and Cosmetic Act.

(iii) An individual convicted of a crime enumerated in section 6105.

(iv) An individual who, within the past ten years, has been adjudicated delinquent for a crime enumerated in section 6105 or for an offense under the Controlled Substance, Drug, device and Cosmetic Act.

(v) An individual who is not of sound mind or who has ever been committed to a mental institution.

(vi) An individual who is addicted to or is an unlawful user of marijuana or a stimulant, depressant or narcotic drug.

(vii) An individual who is a habitual drunkard.

(viii) An individual who is charged with or has been convicted of a crime punishable by imprisonment for a term exceeding one year except as provided for in section 6123 (relating to waiver of disability or pardons).

(ix) A resident of another state who does not possess a current license or permit or similar document to carry a firearm issued by that state if a license is provided for by the laws of that state, as published annually in the federal register by the Bureau of Alcohol, Tobacco and Firearms of the Department of the Treasury under 18 U.S.C. section 921 (a) (19) (relating to definitions).

(x) An alien who is illegally in the United States.

(xi) An individual who has been discharged from the armed forces of the United States under dishonorable conditions.

(xii) An individual who is a fugitive from justice.

(xiii) An individual who is otherwise prohibited from possessing, using, manufacturing, controlling, purchasing, selling or transferring a firearm as provided by section 6105.

(2) The license shall bear the name, address, date of birth, race, sex, citizenship, social security number, height, weight, color of hair, color of eyes and signature of the licensee; the signature of the sheriff issuing the license; the reason for issuance; and the period of validation. The sheriff may also require a photograph of the licensee on the license. The original license shall be issued to the applicant. The first copy of the license shall be forwarded to the commissioner within seven days of the date of issue, and a second copy shall be retained by the issuing authority for a period of six years.

(f) Term of license.

(1) A license to carry a firearm issued under subsection (e) shall be valid throughout this Commonwealth for a period of five years unless sooner revoked.

(2) At least 60 days prior to the expiration of each license, the issuing sheriff shall send to the licensee an application for renewal of license. Failure to receive a renewal application shall not relieve a licensee from the responsibility to renew the license.

(g) Grant or denial of license. Upon the receipt of an application for a license to carry a firearm, the sheriff shall, within 45 days, issue or refuse to issue a license on the basis of the investigation under subsection (d) and the accuracy of the information contained in the application. If the sheriff refuses to issue a license, the sheriff shall notify the applicant in writing of the refusal and the specific reasons. The notice shall be sent by certified mail to the applicant at the address set forth in the application.

(h) Fee. The fee for a license to carry a firearm is $19. This includes a renewal notice processing fee of $1.50. This includes an administrative fee of $5 under section 14 (2) of the act of July 6, 1984 (P.L. 614, No. 127), known as the Sheriff Fee Act. No fee other than that provided by this paragraph or the Sheriff Fee Act may be assessed by the sheriff for the performance of any background check made pursuant to this act. The fee is payable to the sheriff to whom the application is submitted and is payable at the time of application for the license. Except for the administrative fee of $5 under section 14 (2) of the Sheriff Fee Act, all other fees shall be refunded if the application is denied but shall not be refunded if a license is issued and subsequently revoked. A person who sells or attempts to sell a license to carry a firearm for a fee in excess of the amounts fixed under this subsection commits a summary offense.

(i) Revocation. A license to carry firearms may be revoked by the issuing authority for good cause. Notice of revocation shall be in writing and shall state the specific reason for revocation. Notice shall be sent by certified mail, and, at that time, a copy shall be forwarded to the Commissioner. An individual whose license is revoked shall surrender the license to the issuing authority within five days of receipt of the notice. An individual who violates this section commits a summary offense.

(j) Immunity. A sheriff who complies in good faith with this section shall be immune from liability resulting or arising from the action or misconduct with a firearm committed by any individual to whom a license to carry a firearm has been issued.

(k) Reciprocity. The attorney general may enter into reciprocity agreements with other states providing for the mutual recognition of each state's license to carry a firearm.

[18 Pa. C.S. § 6109; Act 17; Act 66, eff. imm.]

SECTION 6122
Proof of License and Exception

(a) General rule. When carrying a firearm concealed on or about one's person or in a vehicle, an individual licensed to carry a firearm shall, upon lawful demand of a law enforcement officer, produce the license for inspection.

(b) Exception. An individual carrying a firearm on or about his person or in a vehicle and claiming an exception under section 6106 (b) (relating to firearms not to be carried without a license) shall, upon lawful demand of a law enforcement officer, produce satisfactory evidence of qualification for exception.

[18 Pa. C.S. § 6122]

SECTION 6110.1
Possession of Firearm by Minor

(a) Firearm. Except as provided in subsection (b), a person under 18 years of age shall not possess or transport a firearm anywhere in this Commonwealth.

(b) Exception. Subsection (a) shall not apply to a person under 18 years of age

(1) who is under the supervision of a parent, grandparent, legal guardian or an adult acting with the expressed consent of the minor's custodial parent or legal guardian and the minor is engaged in lawful activity, including safety training, lawful target shooting, engaging in an organized competition involving the use of a firearm or the firearm is unloaded and the minor is transporting it for a lawful purpose; or

(2) who is lawfully hunting or trapping in accordance with 34 Pa. C.S. (relating to game).

(c) **Responsibility of adult.** Any person who knowingly and intentionally delivers or provides to the minor a firearm in violation of subsection (a) commits a felony of the third degree.

(b) **Forfeiture.** Any firearm in the possession of a person under 18 years of age in violation of this section shall be promptly seized by the arresting law enforcement officer and upon conviction or adjudication of delinquency shall be forfeited or, if stolen, returned to the lawful owner.

[18 Pa. C.S. § 6110.1; Act 17; Act 66, eff. imm.]

SECTION 6302
Sale or Lease of Weapons and Explosives

(a) **Offense defined.** A person is guilty of a misdemeanor of the first degree if he sells or causes to be sold or leases to any person under 18 years of age any deadly weapon, cartridge, gunpowder, or other similar dangerous explosive substance.

(b) **Exception.** The provisions of subsection (a) shall not prohibit hunting by minors under 18 years of age permitted under Title 34 (relating to game).

[18 Pa. C.S. § 6302]

SECTION 6111
Sale or Transfer of Firearms

(a) **Time and manner of delivery.**

    (1) Except as provided in paragraph (2), no seller shall deliver a firearm to the purchaser or transferee thereof until 48 hours shall have elapsed from the time of the application for the purchase thereof, and, when delivered, the firearm shall be securely wrapped and shall be unloaded.

    (2) Thirty days after publication in the Pennsylvania bulletin that the instantaneous criminal history records check system has been established in accordance with the Brady Handgun Violence Prevention Act (Public Law 103-159, 18 U.S.C. § 921 et seq.), no seller shall deliver a firearm to the purchaser thereof until the provisions of this section have been satisfied, and, when delivered, the firearm shall be securely wrapped and shall be unloaded.

(b) **Duty of seller.** No licensed importer, licensed manufacturer or licensed dealer shall sell or deliver any firearm to another person, other than a licensed importer, licensed manufacturer, licensed dealer or licensed collector, until the conditions of subsection (a) have been satisfied and until he has:

(1) For purposes of a firearm as defined in section 6102 (relating to definitions), obtained a completed application/record of sale from the potential buyer or transferee to be filled out in triplicate, the original copy to be sent to the Pennsylvania State Police, postmarked via first class mail, within 14 days of the sale, one copy to be retained by the licensed importer, licensed manufacturer or licensed dealer and one copy to be retained by the purchaser or transferee. The form of this application/record of sale shall be no more than one page in length and shall be promulgated by the Pennsylvania State Police and provided by the licensed importer, licensed manufacturer or licensed dealer. The application/record of sale shall include the name, address, birthdate, gender, race, physical description and Social Security number of the purchaser or transferee, the date of the application and the caliber, length of barrel, make, model and manufacturer's number of the firearm to be purchased or transferred.

(1.1) For purposes of a firearm which exceeds the barrel and related lengths set forth in section 6102, obtained a completed application/record of sale from the potential buyer or transferee to be filled out in triplicate, the original copy to be sent to the Pennsylvania State Police, postmarked via first class mail, within 14 days of sale, one copy to be retained by the licensed importer, licensed manufacturer or licensed dealer and one copy to be retained by the purchaser or transferee. The form of the application/record of sale shall be no more than one page in length and shall be promulgated by the Pennsylvania State Police and provided by the licensed importer, licensed manufacturer or licensed dealer. For purposes of conducting the criminal history, juvenile delinquency and mental health records background check which shall be completed within ten days of receipt of the information from the dealer, the application/record of sale shall include the name, address, birthdate, gender, race, physical description and Social Security number of the purchaser or transferee and the date of application. No information regarding the type of firearm need be included other than an indication that the firearm exceeds the barrel lengths set forth in section 6102. Unless it has been discovered pursuant to a criminal history, juvenile delinquency and mental health records background check that the potential purchaser or transferee is prohibited from possessing a firearm pursuant to section 6105 (relating to persons not to possess, use, manufacture, control, sell or transfer firearms), no information on the application/record of sale provided pursuant to this subsection shall be retained as precluded by section 6111.4 (relating to registration of firearms) by the Pennsylvania State Police either through retention of the application/record of sale or by entering the information onto a computer, and further an application/record of sale received by the Pennsylvania State Police pursuant to this subsection shall be destroyed within 72 hours of the completion of the criminal history, juvenile delinquency and mental health records background check.

(1.2) Fees collected under paragraph (3) and section 6111.2 (relating to firearm sales surcharge) shall be transmitted to the Pennsylvania State Police within 14 days of collection.

(1.3) In addition to the criminal penalty under section 6119 (relating to violation penalty), any person who knowingly and intentionally maintains or fails to destroy any information submitted to the Pennsylvania State Police for purposes of a background check pursuant to paragraphs (1.1) and (1.4) shall be subject to a civil penalty of up to $250 per entry or failure to destroy.

(1.4) Prior to January 1, 1997, and following implementation of the instantaneous records check by the Pennsylvania State Police on or before October 11, 1999, no application/record of sale shall be completed for the purchase or transfer of a firearm which exceeds the barrel lengths set forth in section 6102. A statement shall be submitted by the dealer to the Pennsylvania State Police, postmarked via first class mail, within 14 days of the sale, containing the number of firearms sold which exceed the barrel and related lengths set forth in section 6102, the amount of surcharge and other fees remitted and a list of the unique approval numbers given pursuant to paragraph (4) together with a statement that the background checks have been performed on the firearms contained in the statement. The form of the statement relating to performance of background checks shall be promulgated by the Pennsylvania State Police.

(2) Inspected photo identification of the potential purchaser or transferee, including, but not limited to, a driver's license, official Pennsylvania photo identification card or official government photo identification card. In the case of a potential buyer or transferee who is a member of a recognized religious sect or community whose tenets forbid or discourage the taking of photographs of members of that sect or community, a seller shall accept a valid-without-photo driver's license or a combination of documents, as prescribed by the Pennsylvania State Police, containing the applicant's name, address, date of birth and the signature of the applicant.

(3) Requested, by means of a telephone call, that the Pennsylvania State Police, conduct a criminal history, juvenile delinquency history and a mental health record check. The requester shall be charged a fee equivalent to the cost of providing the service but not to exceed $2 per buyer or transferee.

(4) Received a unique approval number for that inquiry from the Pennsylvania State Police and recorded the date and the number on the application/record of sale form.

(5) Issued a receipt containing the information from paragraph (4), including the unique approval number of the purchaser. This receipt shall be prima facie evidence of the purchaser's or transferee's compliance with the provisions of this section.

(6) Unless it has been discovered pursuant to a criminal history, juvenile delinquency and mental health records background check that the potential purchaser or transferee is prohibited from possessing a firearm pursuant to section 6105, no information received via telephone following the implementation of the instantaneous background check system from a purchaser or transferee who has received a unique approval number shall be retained by the Pennsylvania State Police.

(c) Duty of other persons. Any person who is not a licensed importer, manufacturer or dealer and who desires to sell or transfer a firearm to another unlicensed person shall do so only upon the place of business of a licensed importer, manufacturer, dealer or county sheriff's office, the latter of whom shall follow the procedure set forth in this section as if he were the seller of the firearm. The provisions of this section shall not apply to transfers between spouses or to transfers between a parent and child or to transfers between grandparent and grandchild.

(d) Defense. Compliance with the provisions of this section shall be a defense to any criminal complaint under the laws of this Commonwealth arising from the sale or transfer of any firearm.

(e) Nonapplicability of section. This section shall not apply to the following:

(1) Any firearm manufactured on or before 1898.

(2) Any firearm with a matchlock, flintlock or percussion cap type of ignition system.

(3) Any replica of any firearm described in paragraph (1) if the replica:

(i) is not designed or redesigned to use rimfire or conventional center fire fixed ammunition; or

(ii) uses rimfire or conventional center fire fixed ammunition which is no longer manufactured in the United States and which is not readily available in the ordinary channels of commercial trade.

(f) Application of section.

(1) For the purposes of this section only, except as provided by paragraph (2), "firearm" shall mean any weapon which is designed to or may readily be converted to expel any projectile by the action of an explosive or the frame or receiver of any such weapon.

(2) The provisions contained in subsections (a) (relating to the time and manner of delivery) and (c) (relating to the duty of other persons) shall only apply to pistols or revolvers with a barrel length of less than 15 inches, any shotgun with a barrel length of less than 18 inches, or any rifle with a barrel length of less than 16 inches or any firearm with an overall length of less than 26 inches.

(3) The provisions contained in subsection (a) shall not apply to any law enforcement officer whose current identification as a law enforcement officer shall be construed as a valid license to carry a firearm or any person who possesses a valid license to carry a firearm under section 6109 (relating to licenses).

(4)   (i) The provisions of subsection (a) shall not apply to any person who presents to the seller or transferor a written statement, issued by the offical described in subparagraph (iii) during the ten-day period ending on the date of the most recent proposal of such transfer or sale by the transferee or purchaser stating that the transferee or purchaser requires access to a firearm because of a threat to the life of the transferee or purchaser or any member of the household of that transferee or purchaser.

   (ii) The issuing official shall notify the applicant's local police authority that such a statement has been issued. In counties of the first class the chief of police shall notify the police station or substation closest to the applicant's residence.

   (iii) The statement issued under subparagraph (ii) shall be issued by the district attorney, or his designee, of the county of residence if the transferee or purchaser resides in a municipality where there is no chief of police. Otherwise, the statement shall be issued by the chief of police in the municipality in which the purchaser or transferee resides.

(g) Penalties.

(1) Any person, licensed dealer, licensed manufacturer or licensed importer who knowingly or intentionally sells, delivers or transfers a firearm in violation of this section commits a misdemeanor of the second degree.

(2) Any person, licensed dealer, licensed manufacturer or licensed importer who knowingly or intentionally sells, delivers or transfers a firearm under circumstances intended to provide a firearm to any person, or transferee who is unqualified or ineligible to control, posses or use a firearm under this chapter commits a felony of the third degree and shall, in addition, be subject to revocation of the license to sell firearms for a period of three years.

(3) Any person, licensed dealer, licensed manufacturer or licensed importer who knowingly and intentionally requests a criminal history, juvenile delinquency or mental health record check from the Pennsylvania State Police under this chapter for any purpose other than compliance with this chapter or knowingly and intentionally disseminates any criminal history, juvenile delinquency or mental health record information to any person other than the subject of the information commits a felony of the third degree.

(4) Any person, purchaser or transferee who, in connection with the purchase, delivery or transfer of a firearm under this chapter, knowingly and intentionally makes any materially false oral or written statement or willfully furnishes or exhibits any false identification intended or likely to deceive the seller, licensed dealer or licensed manufacturer commits a felony of the third degree.

(5) Notwithstanding section 306 (relating to liability for conduct of another; complicity) or any other statute to the contrary, any person, licensed importer, licensed dealer or licensed manufacturer who knowingly and intentionally sells, delivers or transfers a firearm in violation of this chapter who has reason to believe that the firearm is intended to be used in the commission of a crime or attempt to commit a crime shall be criminally liable for such crime or attempted crime.

(6) Notwithstanding any act or statute to the contrary, any person, licensed importer, licensed manufacturer or licensed dealer who knowingly and intentionally sells or delivers a firearm in violation of this chapter who has reason to believe that the firearm is intended to be used in the commission of a crime or attempt to commit a crime shall be liable in the amount of the civil judgment for injuries suffered by any person so injured by such crime or attempted crime.

(h) Subsequent violation penalty.

(1) A second or subsequent violation of this section shall be a felony of the second degree and shall be punishable by a mandatory minimum sentence of imprisonment of five years. A second or subsequent offense shall also result in permanent revocation of any license to sell, import or manufacture a firearm.

(2) Notice of the applicability of this subsection to the defendant shall not be required prior to conviction, but reasonable notice of the Commonwealth's intention to proceed under this section shall be provided after conviction and before sentencing. The applicability of this section shall be determined at sentencing. The court

shall consider evidence presented at trial, shall afford the Commonwealth and the defendant an opportunity to present necessary additional evidence, and shall determine, by a preponderance of the evidence, if this section is applicable.

(3) There shall be no authority for a court to impose on a defendant to which this subsection is applicable a lesser sentence than provided for in paragraph (1), to place the defendant on probation or to suspend sentence. Nothing in this section shall prevent the sentencing court from imposing a sentence greater than that provided in this section. Sentencing guidelines promulgated by the Pennsylvania commission on sentencing shall not supersede the mandatory sentences provided in this section.

(4) If a sentencing court refuses to apply this subsection where applicable, the Commonwealth shall have the right to appellate review of the action of the sentencing court. The appellate court shall vacate the sentence and remand the case to the sentencing court for imposition of a sentence in accordance with this section if it finds that the sentence was imposed in violation of this subsection.

(i) Confidentiality. Information furnished by a potential purchaser or transferee under this section or any applicant for a license to carry a firearm as provided by section 6109 shall be confidential and not subject to public disclosures.

[18 Pa. C.S. § 6111; Act 17; Act 66 - see Section 11, below]

─── SECTION 11 of ACT 66 ───

Until such time as the amendatory provisions of 18 Pa. C.S. § 6111 (b) which are set forth in this act take effect, the Pennsylvania State Police shall only apply the provision of 18 Pa. C.S. § 6111 (b) (1) as it ixisted on the day prior to the effective date of this act to any firearm which meets the standards in the definition of "firearm" set forth in 18 Pa. C.S. § 6102.

[Author's Note: The addition of 18 Pa. C.S. § 6111 (b) (1.1) takes effect on January 1, 1997, the amendments of § 6111 (b), (e), (f), ande (g) are eff. imm.]

─── SECTION 6126 ───
Firearms Background Check Advisory Committee

(a) Establishment. There is hereby established the Firearms Background Check Advisory Committee which shall consist of six members as follows:

(1) The Governor or a designee.

(2) The Attorney General or a designee.

(3) The Majority Leader of the Senate or a designee.

(4) The Minority Leader of the Senate or a designee.

(5) The Majority Leader of the House of Representatives or a designee.

(6) The Minority Leader of the House of Representatives or a designee.

(b) Duties. To facilitate compliance with this chapter and the intent threof, the Firearms Background Check Advisory Committee shall, as follows:

    (1) Review the operations and procedures of the Pennsylvania State Police relating to the implementation and administration of the criminal history, juvenile delinquency and mental health records background checks.

    (2) Advise the Pennsylvania State Police relating to the development and maintenance of the instantaneous records check system.

    (3) Provide annual reports to the Governor and the General Assembly on the advisory committee's findings and recommendations, including discussions concerning conformance with the Preamble of the act of June 13, 1995 (1st Sp. Sess., P.L., No. 17), entitled, "An act amending Titles 18 (Crimes and Offenses) and 42 (Judiciary and Judicial Procedure) of the Pennsylvania Consolidated Statutes, further providing for the possession of firearms; establishing a selected Statewide juvenile offender registry; and making an appropriation."

(c) Terms. Members or their designees shall serve a term of office concurrent with the term of office for which the member was elected. Any vacancy shall be filled by the appointing authority.

(d) Chairperson. The Governor shall appoint the chairperson of the advisory committee.

(e) Expiration. This section shall expire July 1, 2001, or at the end of two years following the implementation of the instant records check, whichever is sooner.

[18 Pa. C.S. § 6126 added by Act 66, eff. July 1. 1996.]

SECTION 6111.1
Pennsylvania State Police

(a) Administration. The Pennsylvania State Police shall have the responsibility to administer the provisions of this chapter.

Duty of Pennsylvania State Police.

    (i) Upon receipt of a request for a criminal history, juvenile delinquency history and mental health record check of the potential purchaser or transferee, the Pennsylvania State Police shall immediately, during the licensee's call or by return call, forthwith:

        (i) Review the Pennsylvania State Police criminal history and fingerprint records to determine if the potential purchaser or transferee is prohibited from receipt or possession of a firearm under federal or state law;

        (ii) Review the juvenile delinquency and mental health records of the Pennsylvania State Police to determine whether the potential purchaser or transferee is prohibited from receipt or possession of a firearm under federal or state law; and

    (iii) Inform the licensee making the inquiry either:

        (a) that the potential purchase or transfer is prohibited; or

        (b) provide the licensee with a unique approval number.

(2) In the event of electronic failure or similar event beyond the control of the Pennsylvania State Police, the Pennsylvania State Police shall immediately notify the requesting licensee of the reason for and estimated length of the delay. If the failure or event lasts for a period exceeding 48 hours, the dealer shall not be subject to any penalty for failure to complete an instantaneous records check for the remainder of the failure or similar event, but the dealer shall obtain a completed application/record of sale following the provisions of section 6111 (b) (1) and (1.1) (relating to sale or transfer of firearms) as if an instantaneous records check has not been established for any sale or transfer of a firearm for the purpose of a subsequent background check.

(3) The Pennsylvania State Police shall fully comply, execute and enforce the directives of this section within four years of the enactment of this subsection.

(4) The Pennsylvania State Police and any local law enforcement agency shall make all reasonable efforts to determine the lawful owner of any firearm confiscated by the Pennsylvania State Police or any local law enforcement agency and return said firearm to its lawful owner if the owner is not otherwise prohibited from possessing the firearm. When a court of law has determined that the Pennsylvania State Police or any local law enforcement agency have failed to exercise the duty under this subsection, reasonable attorney fees shall be awarded to any lawful owner of said firearm who has sought judicial enforcement of this subsection.

(c) **Establish a telephone number.** The Pennsylvania State Police shall establish a telephone number which shall be operational seven days a week between the hours of 8 a.m. and 10 p.m. local time for purposes of responding to inquiries as described in this section from licensed manufacturers, licensed importers and licensed dealers. The Pennsylvania State Police shall employ and train such personnel as are necessary to administer expeditiously the provisions of this section.

(d) **Distribution.** The Pennsylvania State Police shall provide, without charge, summaries of uniform firearm laws and firearm safety brochures pursuant to section 6125 (relating to distribution of uniform firearm laws and firearm safety brochures).

(e) Challenge to records. Any person who is denied the right to receive, sell, transfer, possess, carry, manufacture or purchase a firearm as a result of the procedures established by this section may challenge the accuracy of that person's criminal history, juvelile delinquency history or mental health record under the procedures of Chapter 91 (relating to criminal history record information).

(f) Notification of mental health commitment. Notwithstanding any statute to the contrary, judges of the Courts of Common Pleas shall notify the Pennsylvania State Police on a form developed by the Pennsylvania State Police of the identity of any individual who has been adjudicated incompetent or who has been involuntarily committed to a mental institution for inpatient care and treatment under the act of June 9, 1976 (P.L. 817, No. 143), known as the Mental Health Procedures Act, or who has been involuntarily treated as described in section 6105 (c) (4) (relating to persons not to possess, use, manufacture, control, sell or transfer firearms). The notification shall be transmited by the judge to the Pennsylvania State Police within seven days of the adjudication, commitment or treatment.

(g) Review by court.

(1) Upon receipt of a copy of the order of a court of competent jurisdiction which vacates a final order or an involuntary certification issued by a mental health review officer, the Pennsylvania State Police shall expunge all records of the involuntary treatment received under subsection (f).

(2) A person who is involuntarily committed pursuant to section 302 of the Mental Health Procedures Act may petition the court to review the sufficiency of the evidence upon which the commitment was based. If the court determines that the evidence upon which the involuntary commitment was based was insufficient, the court shall order that the record of the commitment submitted to the Pennsylvania State Police be expunged. A petition filed under this subsection shall toll the 60-day period set forth under section 6105 (a) (2).

(3) The Pennsylvania State Police shall expunge all records of an involuntary commitment of an individual who is discharged from a mental health facility based upon the initial review by the physician occurring within two hours of arrival under section 302 (b) of the Mental Health Procedures Act and the physician's determination that no severe mental disability existed pursuant to section 302 (b) of the Mental Health Procedures Act. The physician shall provide signed confirmation of the determination of the lack of severe mental disability following the initial examination under section 302 (b) of the Mental Health Procedures Act to the Pennsylvania State Police.

(h) Juvenile Registry.

(1) The contents of law enforcement records and files compiled under 42 Pa. C.S. § 6308 (relating to law enforcement records) concerning a child shall not be disclosed to the public except if the child is 14 years of age or older at the time of the alleged conduct and if any of the following apply:

(i) The child has been adjudicated delinquent by a court as a result of an act or acts which constitute any offense enumerated in section 6105

(ii) A petition alleging delinquency has been filed by a law enforcement agency alleging that the child has committed an act or acts which constitute an offense enumerated in section 6105 and the child previously has been adjudicated delinquent by a court as a result of an act or acts which included the elements of one of such crimes.

(2) Notwithstanding any provision of this subsection, the contents of law enforcement records and files concerning any child adjudicated delinquent for the commission of any criminal activity described in paragraph (1) shall be recorded in the registry of the Pennsylvania State Police for the limited purposes of this chapter.

(i) Reports. The Pennsylvania State Police shall annually compile and report to the General Assembly, on or before December 31, the following information for the previous year:

(1) Number of firearm sales, including the types of firearms;
(2) Number of applications for sale of firearms denied; number of challenges of the denials; and number of final reversals of initial denials;
(3) Summary of the Pennsylvania State Police's activities, including the average time taken to complete a criminal history, juvenile delinquency history or mental health record check; and
(4) Uniform crime reporting statistics compiled by the Pennsylvania State Police based on the national incident-based reporting system.

(j) Other criminal information. The Pennsylvania State Police shall be authorized to obtain any crime statistics necessary for the purposes of this chapter from any local law enforcement agency.

(1) Delinquency and mental health records. The provisions of this section which relate to juvenile delinquency and mental health records checks shall be applicable when the data has been made available to the Pennsylvania State Police but not later than October 11, 1999.

(2) Records check. The provisions of this section which relate to the instantaneous records check conducted by telephone shall be applicable 30 days following notice by the Pennsylvania state Police pursuant to subsection (a) (2).

(k) Definition. For the purposes of this section only, the term "firearm" shall have the same meaning as in § 6111.2 (relating to firearm sales surcharge). *[18 Pa. C.S. § 6111.1; Act 17; Act 66, eff. imm.]*

SECTION 6111.2
Firearm Sales Surcharge

(a) Surcharge imposed. There is hereby imposed on each sale of a firearm subject to tax under article II of the act of March 4, 1971 (P.L. 6, No. 2), known as the Tax Reform Code of 1971, an additional surcharge of $3. This shall be referred to as the Firearm Sale Surcharge. All moneys received from this surcharge shall be deposited in the Firearm Instant Records Check Fund.

(b) Increases or decreases. Five years from the effective date of this subsection, and every five years thereafter, the Pennsylvania State Police shall provide such information as necessary to the legislative budget and finance committee for the purpose of reviewing the need to increase or decrease the instant check fee. The committee shall issue a report of its findings and recommendations to the general assembly for a statutory change in the fee.

(c) Revenue sources. Funds received under the provisions of this section and section 6111 (b) (3), as estimated and certified by the Secretary of Revenue, shall be deposited within five days of the end of each quarter into the fund.

(d) Definition. As used in this section only, the term "firearm" shall mean any weapon which is designed to or may readily be converted to expel any projectile by the action of an explosion or the frame or receiver of any such weapon.
[18 Pa. C.S. § 6111.2; Act 17; Act 66, eff. imm.]

SECTION 6111.3
Firearm Instant Records Check Fund

(a) Establishment. The firearm ownership fund is hereby established as a restricted account in the state treasury, separate and apart from all other public money or funds of the Commonwealth, to be appropriated annually by the general assembly, for use in carrying out the provisions of section 6111 (relating to firearm ownership).

(b) Source. The source of the fund shall be moneys collected and transferred under section 6111.2 (relating to firearm sales surcharge) and moneys collected and transferred under section 6111 (b) (3) and 6113 (d) (relating to licensing of   dealers).
[18 Pa. C.S. § 6111.3; Act 17; Act 66, eff. imm.]

SECTION 6111.4
Registration of Firearms

Notwithstanding any section of this chapter to the contrary, nothing in this chapter shall be construed to allow any government or law enforcement agency or any agent thereof to create, maintain or operate any registry of firearm ownership within this Commonwealth. For the purposes of this section only, the term "firearm" shall include any weapon that is designed to or may readily be converted to expel any projectile by the action of an explosive or the frame or receiver of any such weapon.
[18 Pa. C.S. § 6111.4; Act 17]

SECTION 6111.5
Rules and Regulations

The Pennsylvania State Police shall, in the manner provided by law, promulgate the rules and regulations necessary to carry out this chapter, including regulations to ensure the identity, confidentiality and security of all records and data provided pursuant hereto.
[18 Pa. C.S. § 6111.5; Act 17]

SECTION 6112
Retail Dealer Required to be Licensed

No retail dealer shall sell, or otherwise transfer or expose for sale or transfer, or have in his possession with intent to sell or transfer, any firearm without being licensed as provided in this subchapter.
[18 Pa. C.S. § 6112; Act 17]

SECTION 6113
Licensing of Dealers

(a) General Rule. The chief or head of any police force or police department of a city, and, elsewhere, the sheriff of the county, shall grant to reputable applicants licenses, in form prescribed by the Pennsylvania State Police, effective for not more than three years from date of issue, permitting the licensee to sell firearms direct to the consumer, subject to the following conditions in addition to those specified in section 6111 (relating to sale or transfer of firearms), for breach of any of which the license shall be forfeited and the licensee subject to punishment as provided in this subchapter:

(1) The business shall be carried on only upon the premises designated in the license or at a lawful gun show or meet.

(2) The license, or a copy thereof, certified by the issuing authority, shall be displayed on the premises where it can easily be read.

(3) No firearm shall be sold in violation of any provision of this subchapter.

(4) No firearm shall be sold under any circumstances unless the purchaser is personally known to the seller or shall present clear evidence of the purchaser's identity.

(5) A true record in triplicate shall be made of every firearm sold, in a book kept for the purpose, the form of which may be prescribed by the Pennsylvania State Police, and shall be personally signed by the purchaser and by the person effecting the sale, each in the presence of the other, and shall contain the information required by section 6111.

(6) No firearm as defined in section 6102 (relating to definitions) shall be displayed in any part of any premises where it can readily be seen from the outside. In the event that the Commissioner of the Pennsylvania State Police shall find a clear and present danger to public safety within this Commonwealth or any area thereof, firearms shall be stored and safeguarded pursuant to regulations to be established by the Pennsylvania State Police by the licensee during the hours when the licensee is closed for business.

(7) The dealer shall possess all applicable current revenue licenses.

(b) Fee. The fee for issuing said license shall be $30 shich fee shall be paid into the county treasury.

(c) Revocation. Any license granted under subsection (a) of this section may be revoked for cause by the person issuing the same, upon written notice to the holder thereof.

(d) Definitions. For the purposes of this section only unless otherwise specifically provided, the term "firearm" shall include any weapon that is designed to or may readily be converted to expel any projectile by the action of an explosive or the frame or receiver of any such weapon.
[18 Pa. C.S. § 6113; Act 17; Act 66, eff. imm.]

SECTION 6114
Judicial Review

The action of the chief of police, sheriff, county treasurer or other officer under this subchapter shall be subject to judicial review in the manner and within the time provided by 2 Pa. C.S. Ch. 7 Subch. b (relating to judicial review of local agency action). A judgment sustaining a refusal to grant a license shall not bar, after one year, a new application; nor shall a judgment in favor of the petitioner prevent the defendant from thereafter revoking or refusing to renew such license for any proper cause which may thereafter occur. The court shall have full power to dispose of all costs. *[18 Pa. C.S. § 6114; Act 17]*

─────────── **SECTION 6115** ───────────

Loans On, or Lending or Giving Firearms Prohibited

(a) Offense defined. No person shall make any loan secured by mortgage, deposit or pledge of a firearm nor, except as provided in subsection (b), shall any person lend or give a firearm to another or otherwise deliver a firearm contrary to the provisions of this subchapter.

(b) Exception.

(1) Subsection (a) shall not apply if any of the following apply:

(iii) The person who receives the firearm is engaged in a hunter safety program certified by the Pennsylvania Game Commission or a firearm training program or competition sanctioned or approved by the National Rifle Association.

(iv) The person who receives the firearm meets all of the following:

(a) is under 18 years of age.

(b) pursuant to section 6110.1 (relating to possession of firearm by minor) is under the supervision, guidance and instruction of a responsible individual who:

(i) is 21 years of age or older; and

(ii) is not prohibited from owning or possessing a firearm under section 6105 (relating to persons not to possess, use, manufacture, control, sell or transfer firearms.)

(v) The person who receives the firearm is lawfully hunting or trapping and is in compliance with the provisions of 34 Pa. C.S. (relating to game).

(vi) A bank or other chartered lending institution is able to adequately secure firearms in its possession.

(2) Nothing in this section shall be construed to prohibit the transfer of a firearm under 20 Pa. C.S. Ch. 21 (relating to intestate succession) or by bequest if the individual receiving the firearm is not precluded from owning or possessing a firearm under section 6105.

(3) Nothing in this section shall be construed to prohibit the loaning or giving of a firearm to another in one's dwelling or place of business if the firearm is retained within the dwelling or place of business. *[18 Pa. C.S. § 6115; Act 17]*

SECTION 6116
False Evidence of Identity

In addition to any other panalty provided in this chapter, the furnishing of false information or offering false evidence of identity is a violation of section 4904 (relating to unsworn falsification to authorities).
[18 Pa. C.S. § 6116; Act 17]

SECTION 6117
Altering or Obliterating Marks of Identification

(a) **Offense defined.** No person shall change, alter, remove, or obliterate the manufacturer's number integral to the frame or receiver of any firearm which shall have the same meaning as provided in section 6105 (relating to persons not to possess, use, manufacture, sell or transfer firearms).

(b) **Presumption.** Possession of any firearm upon which any such mark shall have been changed, altered, remofed or obliterated shall be prima facie evidence that the possessor has changed, altered, removed or obliterated the same.

(c) **Penalty.** A violation of this section constitutes a felony of the second degree.

(d) **Appellate review.** If a sentencing court refuses to apply this section where applicable, the Commonwealth shall have the right to appellate review of the action of the sentencing court. The appellate court shall vacate the sentence and remand the case to the sentencing court for imposition of a sentence in accordance with this section if it finds that the sentence was imposed in violation of this section
[18 Pa. C.S. § 6117; Act 17; Act 66, eff. imm.]

SECTION 6118
Antique Firearms

(a) **General rule.** This subchapter shall not apply to antique firearms.

(b) **Exception.** Subsection (a) shall not apply to the extent that such antique firearms, reproductions or replicas of firearms are concealed weapons as provided in section 6106 (relating to firearms not to be carried without a license), nor shall it apply to the provisions of section 6105 (relating to persons not to possess, use, manufacture, control, sell or transfer firearms) if such antique firearms, reproductions or replicas of firearms ar suitable for use.

(c) **Definition.** As used in this section, the term "antique firearm" means:

(1) Any firearm with a matchlock, flintlock or percussion cap type of ignition system.

(2) Any, firearm manufactured on or before 1898.

(3) Any replica of any firearm described in paragraph (2) if such replica:

(i) is not designed or redesigned for using rimfire or conventional center fire fixed ammunition; or

(ii) uses rimfire or conventional center fire fixed ammunition which is no longer manufactured in the United States and which is not readily available in the ordinary channels of commercial trade.

[18 Pa. C.S. § 6118; Act 17; Act 66, eff. imm.]

SECTION 6119
Violation Penalty

Except as otherwise specifically provided, an offense under this subchapter constitutes a misdemeanor of the first degree.

SECTION 6125
Distribution of Uniform Firearm Laws and Firearm Safety Brochures

It shall be the duty of the Pennsylvania State Police beginning January 1, 1996, to distribute to every licensed firearm dealer in this Commonwealth firearms safety brochures at no cost to the dealer. The brochures shall be written by the Pennsylvania State Police, with the cooperation of the Pennsylvania Game Commission, and shall include a summary of the major provisions of this subchapter, including, but not limited to, the duties of the sellers and purchasers and the transferees of firearms. The brochure or a copy thereof shall be provided without charge to each purchaser.

[18 Pa. C.S. § 6125; Act 17; Act 66, eff. imm.]

SECTION 6308
Law Enforcement Records

* * *

(d) Pennsylvania State Police Registry.

(1) The contents of law enforcement records and files concerning a child shall not be disclosed to the public except if the child is 14 years of age or older at the time of the alleged conduct and if any of the following apply:

(i) The child has been adjudicated delinquent by a court as a result of any offense enumerated in 18 Pa. C.S. § 6105 (relating to persons not to possess, use, manufacture, control, sell or transfer firearms).

(ii) A petition alleging delinquency has been filed by a law enforcement agency alleging that the child has committed any offense enumerated in 18 Pa. C.S. § 6105 and the child previously has been adjudicated delinquent by a court as a result of an actor acts which included the elements of one of such crimes.

(iii) The child is a dangerous juvenile offender.

[42 Pa. C.S. § 6308; Act 17; Act 66, eff. imm.]

SECTION 6121
Certain Bullets Prohibited

(a) Offense defined. It is unlawful for any person to possess, use or attempt to use a KTW teflon-coated bullet or other armor-piercing ammunition while committing or attempting to commit a crime of violence as defined in section 6102 (relating to definitions).

(b) Grading. An offense under this section constitutes a felony of the third degree.

(c) Sentencing. Any person who is convicted in any court of this Commonwealth of a crime of violence and who uses or carries, in the commission of that crime, a firearm loaded with KTW ammunition or any person who violates this section shall, in addition to the punishment provided for the commission of the crime, be sentenced to a term of imprisonment for not less than five years. Notwithstanding any other provision of law, the court shall not suspend the sentence of any person convicted of a crime subject to this subsection nor place him on probation nor shall the term of imprisonment run concurrently with any other term of imprisonment including that imposed for the crime in which the KTW ammunition was being used or carried. No person sentenced under this subsection shall be eligible for parole.

(d) Definition. As used in this section the term "armor-piercing ammunition" means ammunition which, when or if fired from any firearm as defined in section 6102 that is used or attempted to be used in violation of subsection (a) under the test procedure of the National Institute of Law Enforcement and Criminal Justice Standard for the Ballistics Resistance of Police Body Armor promulgated   December 1978, is determined to be capable of penetrating bullet-resistant   apparel or body armor meeting the requirements of type IIA of standard NILECJ-STD-0101.01 as formulated by the United States Department of Justice and published in December 1978.
[18 Pa. C.S. § 6121]

SECTION 6303
Sale of Starter Pistols

(a) Offense defined. A person is guilty of a misdemeanor of the first degree if he sells, causes to be sold, gives or furnishes to any person under the age of 18 years, or if he, being under the age of 18 years, purchases, accepts, receives or possesses, any pistol commonly referred to as "starter pistol" specially designed to receive and discharge blank cartridges only or similar pistol.

(b) Exception. Nothing in this section shall prohibit the use of starter pistols for the purpose of starting or officiating at athletic events, use in dramatic productions, or other similar events.
[18 Pa. C.S. § 6303]

SECTION 6304
Sale and Use of Air Rifles

(a) Sale or transfer of air rifles.

(1) It shall be unlawful for any dealer to sell, lend, rent, give, or otherwise transfer an air rifle to any person under the age of 18 years, where the dealer knows, or has reasonable cause to believe, the person to be under 18 years of age, or where such dealer has failed to make reasonable inquiry relative to the age of such person, and such person is under 18 years of age.

(2) It shall be unlawful for any person to sell, give, lend, or otherwise transfer any air rifle to any person under 18 years of age, except where the relationship of parent and child, guardian and ward or adult instructor and pupil exists between such person and the person under 18 years of age.

(b) Carrying or discharging air rifles.

(1) It shall be unlawful for any person under 18 years of age to carry any air rifle on the highways or public lands unless accompanied by an adult, except that a person under 18 years of age may carry such rifle unloaded in a suitable case or securely wrapped.

(2) It shall be unlawful for any person to discharge any air rifle from or across any highway or public land or any public place, except on a properly constructed target range.

(c) Exceptions.

(1) Nothing in this section shall make it unlawful for any person under 18 years of age to have in his possession any air rifle, if it is:

(i) kept within his domicile;

(ii) used by the person under 18 years of age and he is a duly enrolled member of any club, team or society organized for educational purposes and maintaining as part of its facilities or having written permission to use an indoor or outdoor rifle range under the supervision, guidance and instruction of a responsible adult, and then only, if said air rifle is actually being used in connection with the activities of said club, team or society under the supervision of a responsible adult; or

(iii) used in or on any private grounds or residence under circumstances when such air rifle can be fired, discharged or operated in such a manner as not to endanger persons or property, and then only, if it is used in such manner as to prevent the projectile from transversing any grounds or space outside the limits of such grounds or residence.

(1) Nothing in this section shall prohibit sales of air rifles:

    (i) By wholesale dealers or jobbers.
    (ii) To be shipped out of this Commonwealth.
    (iii) To be used at a target range operated in accordance with paragraph (1) of this subsection or by members of the armed services of the United States or veterans' organizations.

(d) **Seizure.** Any law enforcement officer may seize, take, remove or cause to be removed, at the expense of the owner, all air rifles used or offered for sale in violation of this section.

(e) **No preemption.** The provisions of any ordinance enacted by any political subdivision which impose greater restrictions or limitations in respect to the sale and purchase, use or possession of air rifles, than is imposed by this section, shall not be invalidated or affected by this section.

(f) **Grading.** Any dealer violating the provisions of paragraph (a) (1) of this section shall be guilty of a misdemeanor of the third degree. Any person violating any other provision of this section shall be guilty of a summary offense.

(g) **Definitions.** As used in this section the following words and phrases shall have the meanings given to them in this subsection:

> **"Air rifles."** Any air gun, air pistol, spring gun, spring pistol, B-B gun, or any implement that is not a firearm, which impels a pellet of any kind with a force that can reasonably be expected to cause bodily harm.

> **"Dealer."** Any person engaged in the business of selling at retail or renting any air rifles.

[18 Pa. C.S. § 6304]

SECTION 912
Possession of Weapon on School Property

(a) **Definition.** Notwithstanding the definition of "weapon" in section 907 (relating to possessing instruments of crime), "weapon" for purposes of this section shall include but not be limited to any knife, cutting instrument, cutting tool, nunchuck stick, firearm, shotgun, rifle and any other tool, instrument or implement capable of inflicting serious bodily injury.

(b) **Offense defined.** A person commits a misdemeanor of the first degree if he possesses a weapon in the buildings of, on the grounds of, or in any conveyance providing transportation to or from any elementary or second-

113

ary publicly-funded educational institution, any elementary or secondary private school licensed by the Department of Education or any elementary or secondary parochial school.

(c) Defense. It shall be a defense that the weapon is possessed and used in conjunction with a lawful supervised school activity or course or is possessed for other lawful purpose.

[18 Pa. C.S. § 912]

SECTION 913

Possession of Firearm or Other Dangerous Weapon in Court Facility

(a) Offense defined. A person commits an offense if he:

(1) Knowingly possesses a firearm or other dangerous weapon in a court facility or knowingly causes a firearm or other dangerous weapon to be present in a court facility; or

(2) Knowingly possesses a firearm or other dangerous weapon in a court facility with the intent that the firearm or other dangerous weapon be used in the commission of a crime or knowingly causes a firearm or other dangerous weapon to be present in a court facility with the intent that the firearm or other dangerous weapon be used in the commission of a crime.

(b) Grading.

(1) Except as otherwise provided in paragraph (3), an offense under subsection (a) (1) is a misdemeanor of the third degree.

(2) An offense under subsection (a) (2) is a misdemeanor of the first degree.

(3) An offense under subsection (a) (1) is a summary offense if the person was carrying a firearm under section 6106 (b) (relating to firearms not to be carried without a license) or 6109 (relating to licenses) and failed to check the firearm under subsection (e) prior to entering the court facility.

(c) Exceptions. Subsection (a) shall not apply to:

(1) The lawful performance of official duties by an officer, agent or employee of the United States, the Commonwealth or a political subdivision who is authorized by law to engage in or supervise the prevention, detection, investigation or prosecution of any violation of law.

(2) The lawful performance of official duties by a court official.

(3) The carrying of rifles and shotguns by instructors and participants in a course of instruction provided by the Pennsyl-

114

vania Game Commission under 34 Pa. C.S. § 2704 (relating to eligibility for license).

(4) Associations of veteran soldiers and their auxiliaries or members of organized armed forces of the United States or the Commonwealth, including reserve components, when engaged in the performance of ceremonial duties with county approval.

(5) The carrying of a dangerous weapon or firearm unloaded and in a secure wrapper by an attorney who seeks to employ the dangerous weapon or firearm as an exhibit or as a demonstration and who possesses written authorization from the court to bring the dangerous weapon or firearm into the court facility.

(d) **Posting of notice.** Notice of the provisions of subsections (a) and (e) shall be posted conspicuously at each public entrance to each courthouse or other building containing a court facility and each court facility, and no person shall be convicted of an offense under subsection (a) (1) with respect to a court facility if the notice was not so posted at each public entrance to the courthouse or other building containing a court facility and at the court facility, unless the person had actual notice of the provisions of subsection (a).

(e) **Facilities for checking firearms.** Each county shall make available, by July 1, 1996, lockers or similar facilities at no charge or cost for the temporary checking of firearms by persons carrying firearms under section 6106 (b) or 6109. Notice of the location of the facility shall be posted as required under subsection (d).

(f) **Definitions.** As used in this section, the following words and phrases shall have the meanings given to them in this subsection:

"Court facility." The courtroom of a court of record; a courtroom of a community court; the courtroom of a district justice; a courtroom of the Philadelphia Municipal Court; a courtroom of the Pittsburgh Magistrates Court; a courtroom of the Traffic Court of Philadelphia; judge's chambers; witness rooms; jury deliberation rooms; attorney conference rooms; prisoner holding cells; offices of court clerks, the district attorney, the sheriff and probation and parole officers; and any adjoining corridors.

"Dangerous weapon." A bomb, grenade, blackjack, sandbag, metal knuckles, dagger, knife, the blade of which is exposed in an automatic way by switch, push-button, spring mechanism or otherwise, or other implement for the infliction of serious bodily injury which serves no common lawful purpose.

"Firearm." Any weapon, including a starter gun, which will or is designed to expel a projectile or projectiles by the action of an explosion, expansion of gas or escape of gas. The term does not include any device desegned or used exclusively for the firing of stud cartridges, explosive rivets or similar industrial ammunition.

[18 Pa. C.S. § 913; Act 17; Act 66, eff. imm.]

SECTION 6141
Purchase of Firearms in Contiguous States

(a) General Rule. It is lawful for a person residing in this Commonwealth, including a corporation or other business entity maintaining a place of business in this Commonwealth, to purchase or otherwise obtain a rifle or shotgun in a state contiguous to this Commonwealth and to receive or transport such rifle or shotgun into this Commonwealth.

(b) Applicability of section.

(1) This section applies to residents of this Commonwealth who obtain rifles or shotguns from a state contiguous to this Common wealth in compliance with the Gun Control Act of 1968, State laws and local ordinances.

(2) This section shall not apply or be construed to affect in any way the purchase, receipt or transportation of rifles and shotguns by Federally licensed firearms manufacturers, importers, dealers or collectors.

(c) Definitions.

(1) As used in this section the term "a state contiguous to this Commonwealth" means any state having a common border with this Commonwealth.

(2) The other terms used in this section shall have the meanings ascribed to them by Public Law 90-618 known as the "Gun Control Act of 1968."

[18 Pa. C.S. § 6141]

EMERGENCY MANAGEMENT
SECTION 7301
General Authority of Governor

* * *

(f) Additional powers. In addition to any other powers conferred upon the Governor by law, the Governor may:

* * *

(8) Suspend or limit the sale, dispensing or transportation of alcoholic beverages, firearms, explosives and combustibles.

[35 Pa. C.S. § 7301]

116

GAME & WILDLIFE - SPORTING USE OF GUNS

SECTION 102
Definitions

Subject to additional definitions contained in subsequent provisions of this title which are applicable to specific provisions of this title, the following words and phrases when used in this title shall have the meanings given to them in this section unless the context clearly indicates otherwise:

* * *

"Bow." A weapon which propels an arrow, is hand-held, hand-drawn, held in the drawn position by hand or by a hand-held mechanical device and released by hand. The term shall not be construed or interpreted to mean or include what is commonly known as a cross-bow.

* * *

"Contraband." Any game or wildlife, or part or product thereof, or any personal property, including, but not limited to, firearms, traps, boats, decoys, vehicles and attachments and property designed for use or used in hunting and taking game or wildlife, when the game or wildlife, or part or product thereof, or the personal property is held in possession, transported or used or taken in violation of any law, the enforcement or administration of which is vested in the commission. Contraband shall be forfeited to the commission to be disposed of at the discretion of the director.

* * *

"Firearm." An instrument used in the propulsion of shot, shell, bullet or any other object by the action of gunpowder exploded, explosive powder, the expansion of gas or the force of a mechanical device under tension.

> **(1) "Automatic."** Any firearm which discharges more than once with a single pull of the trigger.
>
> **(2) "Semiautomatic."** Any firearm which reloads without aid of the shooter, but fires only once with a single pull of the trigger.

* * *

"Hunt" or "hunting." Any act or furtherance of the taking or killing of any game or wildlife, or any part or product thereof, and includes, but is not limited to, chasing, tracking, calling, pursuing, lying in wait, trapping, shooting at or wounding with any weapon or implement, or using any personal property, including dogs, or the property of others, of any nature, in furtherance of any of these purposes, or aiding, abetting or conspiring with another person in that purpose.

"Loaded firearm." A firearm of any kind which has a live shell or cartridge in either the chamber or magazine.

* * *

[34 Pa. C.S. § 102]

SECTION 712
The Pennsylvania State Police Force

The various members of the Pennsylvania State Police are hereby authorized and empowered:

* * *

(b) To act as game protectors, and as forest, fish, or fire wardens, and for the better performance of such duties,

> Seize all guns, boats, decoys, traps, dogs, game, fish, shooting paraphernalia, or hunting or fishing appliances or devices, used, taken, or had in possession, contrary to the laws of this State. Any article so seized shall be held subject to such disposition as the Executive Director of the Pennsylvania Fish Commission or the Executive Director of the Pennsylvania Game Commission or the Secretary of Environmental Resources may respectively determine.
>
> * * *

[1929, P.L. 177, No. 175, § 712]

SECTION 901
Powers and Duties of Waterways Patrolmen and Deputies

(a) Waterways patrolmen. Every waterways patrolman shall have the power and duty to:

* * *

(4) Carry firearms or other weapons in the performance of their duties.

* * *

(b) Deputy waterways patrolmen. Except for the power conferred by subsection (a) (12), deputy waterways patrolmen may exercise all the powers and perform all the duties conferred by this section on waterways patrolmen.

[30 Pa. C.S. § 901]

SECTION 901
Powers and Duties of Enforcement Officers

Any officer whose duty it is to enforce this title or any officer investigating any alleged violation of this title shall have the power and duty to:

* * *

(4) Carry firearms or other weapons, concealed or otherwise, in the performance of the officer's duties.

* * *

(10) When making an arrest or an investigation or when found in the execution of a search warrant, seize and take possession of all game or wildlife or parts of game or wildlife which have been taken, caught, killed, had or held in possession, and seize all firearms, shooting or hunting paraphernalia, vehicles, boats, conveyances, traps, dogs, decoys, automotive equipment, records, papers, permits, licenses and all contraband or any unlawful device, implement or other appliance used in violation of any of the laws relating to game or wildlife.

* * *

[34 Pa. C.S. § 901]

SECTION 2301
Prima Facie Evidence of Hunting

(a) General rule. For the purpose of this title, any one of the following acts shall constitute prima facie evidence of hunting:

(1) Possession of any firearm, bow and arrow, raptor, trap or other device of any description usuable for the purpose of hunting or taking game or wildlife.

* * *

[34 Pa. C.S. § 2301]

SECTION 928
Disposition of Seized Property

All guns, traps, dogs, boats, vehicles or conveyances, or any device, implement or appliance, and other shooting, hunting, trapping or furtaking paraphernalia seized under this title, where the owner thereof escapes arrest and refuses to present himself and make claim to the property, shall be held for a period of not less than 30 days, after which time the property shall be forwarded to the commission and shall be disposed of at the discretion of the director. The moneys arising from the sale shall be applied to any costs of prosecution accrued and the remainder forfeited to the commission and deposited in the Game Fund.

[34 Pa. C.S. § 928]

SECTION 2126
Unlawful Activities

(a) General rule. It is unlawful for any person while acting under the provisions of this subchapter to:

* * *

(3) Use any firearm except a center fire propelling a single all-lead, lead alloy or expanding bullet or ball to kill or attempt to kill any big game animal.

* * *

[34 Pa. C.S. § 2126]

SECTION 2308
Unlawful Devices and Methods

(a) **General rule.** Except as otherwise provided in this title, it is unlawful for any person to hunt or aid, abet, assist or conspire to hunt any game or wildlife through the use of:

(1) An automatic firearm or similar device.

(2) A semiautomatic rifle or pistol.

(3) A crossbow.

(4) A semiautomatic shotgun or magazine shotgun for hunting or taking small game, furbearers, turkey or unprotected birds unless the shotgun is plugged to a two-shell capacity in the magazine.

(5) Any device operated by air, chemical or gas cylinder by which a projectile of any size or kind can be discharged or propelled.
* * *

(a) **Exceptions.** The provisions of subsection (a) shall not apply to any archery sight or firearm's scope which contains and uses any mechanical, photoelectric, ultraviolet or solar-powered device to solely illuminate the sight or crosshairs within the scope. No archery sight or firearm's scope shall contain or use any device, no matter how powered, to project or transmit any light beam, infrared beam, ultraviolet light beam, radio beam, thermal beam, ultrasonic beam, particle beam or other beam outside the sight or scope onto the target.
* * *
[34 Pa. C.S. § 2308]

SECTION 2310
Unlawful Use of Lights While Hunting

(b) **General rule.** except as set forth in subsection (b), it is unlawful for any person or group of persons to engage in any of the following activities to any degree:

(1) Cast the rays of an artificial light of any kind on any game or wildlife or in an attempt to locate any game or wildlife while on foot, in any vehicle or its attachments, or any watercraft or any airborne craft while in possession of a firearm of any kind, or a bow or arrow, or any implement or device with which any game or wildlife could be killed or taken, even though no game or wildlife is shot at, injured or killed.
* * *

(c) **Penalties.** a violation of this section is a summary offense of the fifth degree. In addition thereto, if any attempt is made to take any game or wildlife or if any firearm or implement capable of killing or wounding game or wildlife is possessed, the person or persons shall be sentenced to the additional penalties of:

(1) For each endangered or threatened species, a fine of $1,000 and forfeiture of the privilege to hunt or take game or wildlife any where within this Commonwealth for a period of ten years.

(2) For each elk or bear, a fine of $800 and forfeiture of the privilege to hunt or take game or wildlife anywhere within this Commonwealth for a period of five years.

(3) For each deer, a fine of $500 and forfeiture of the privilege to hunt or take game or wildlife anywhere within this Commonwealth for a period of three years.

(4) For each bobcat or otter, a fine of $300 and forfeiture of the privilege to hunt or take game or wildlife anywhere within this Commonwealth for a period of three years.

(5) For each turkey or beaver, a fine of $200 and forfeiture of the privilege to hunt or take game or wildlife anywhere within this Commonwealth for a period of two years.

(6) For each other bird or animal, a fine of $100 and forfeiture of the privilege to hunt or take game or wildlife anywhere within this Commonwealth for a period of one year.

(d) Contraband. Any craft or vehicle or attachments thereto, and all artifical lights and any firearm or paraphernalia being unlawfully used, and any game or wildlife unlawfully taken, killed or possessed are contraband. *[34 Pa. C.S. § 2310]*

SECTION 2311
Restrictions on Recreational Spotlighting

(a) Unlawful acts. It is unlawful for any person to cast or to assist any other person in casting the rays of a spotlight, vehicle headlight or any other artificial light of any kind from any vehicle, watercraft, airborne craft or any attachment to such vehicles or crafts.

    * * *

(4) To search for or locate for any purpose any game or wildlife anywhere within this Commonwealth at any time during the antlered deer rifle season and during the antlerless deer rifle season.

    * * *

[34 Pa. C.S. § 2311]

SECTION 2322
Prohibited Devices and Methods

(a) General rule. Except as otherwise provided in this title or commission regulation, no person shall hunt, kill or take or attempt, aid, abet, assist or conspire to hunt, kill or take any big game, except wild turkey, with any of the following devices or methods:

(1) Any device other than a centerfire or muzzle-loading firearm or bow and arrow.

(2) Any automatic or semiautomatic firearm, except that any semi-automatic firearm modified to permit one shell in the chamber and no more than four shells in a magazine may be used by a person who suffered an amputation or lost the total use of one or both hands.

(3) Any firearm propelling more than one projectile per discharge.

* * *

[34 Pa. C.S. § 2322]

SECTION 2325
Cooperation After Lawfully Killing Big Game

(a) **General rule.** Except as provided in section 2301 (b) (relating to lawful cooperation or assistance) and subsection (a.1), it is unlawful for any person who has lawfully killed any big game to hunt for or cooperate with any other person hunting for big game of the same species while carrying a loaded firearm of any kind, a bow and nocked arrow or any other device capable of killing any big game.

* * *

[34 Pa. C.S. § 2325]

SECTION 2363
Trapping Exception for Certain Persons

Except for section 2704 (c) (relating to furtaker's certificate of training), the remaining provisions of this title shall not be construed to prevent or prohibit any person under 12 years of age from trapping furbearers. Persons covered by this section shall not use any firearm other than a .22 caliber rimfire rifle or sidearm and then only when accompanied by an adult.

[34 Pa. C.S. § 2363]

SECTION 2704
Eligibility for License

* * *

(c) **(3)** A certification signed by the applicant on the furtaker's license application that the applicant completed a voluntary trapping course sponsored by the commission or that the applicant has previously hunted or trapped furbearers within the last five years. The provisions of this section shall not apply to those persons under 12 years of age who trap furbearers under the direct supervision of an adult licensed furtaker 18 years of age or older.

* * *

[34 Pa. C.S. § 2704]

SECTION 2501

Hunting or Furtaking Prohibited While Under Influence of Alcohol or Controlled Substance

(a) General rule. It is unlawful to hunt or take game, furbearers or wildlife or aid, abet, assist or conspire to hunt or take game, furbearers or wildlife anywhere in this Commonwealth while in possession of a firearm of any kind or a bow and arrow while under the influence of alcohol or controlled substance, or both.

* * *

[34 Pa. C.S. § 2501]

SECTION 2503

Loaded Firearms in Vehicles

(a) General rule. Except as otherwise provided in this title, it is unlawful for any person to have a firearm of any kind in or on or against any conveyance propelled by mechanical power or its attachments at any time whether or not the vehicle or its attachment is in motion unless the firearm is unloaded.

(b) Exceptions. This section shall not be construed to apply to:

(1) A police officer engaged in the performance of his official duty.

(2) A commission officer engaged in the performance of his duty.

(3) A person carrying a loaded pistol or revolver when in possession of a valid firearms license issued by the chief or head of any police force or the sheriff of a county when the license is issued for protection under 18 Pa. C.S. Ch. 61 Subch. A (relating to Uniform Firearms Act).

(4) Any person as defined in section 2121 (c) (relating to killing game or wildlife to protect property) while on lands they control and when not hunting or trapping for game or wildlife.

(5) Any motorboat or other craft having a motor attached or any sail boat if the motor has been completely shut off or the sail furled and its progress therefrom has ceased.

The exceptions in this subsection do not apply when attempting to locate game or wildlife with an artificial light or when exercising any privileges granted by this title which may be exercised only when not in the possession of a firearm.

(a) Penalty. A violation of this section is a summary offense of the fourth degree if the vehicle is in motion. Otherwise the violation is a summary offense of the fifth degree.

[34 Pa. C.S. § 2503]

SECTION 7727
Additional Limitations on Operation

Except as otherwise permitted under Title 34 (relating to game), no person shall:

(1) Operate or ride in any snowmobile or ATV with any bow and arrows or with any firearm in his possession unless it is unstrung or unloaded.
(2) Drive or pursue any game or wildlife with a snowmobile or an ATV.
[75 Pa. C.S. § 7727]

SECTION 2505
Safety Zones

(a) **General rule.** Except as otherwise provided in this title, it is unlawful for any person, other than the lawful occupant, while hunting game or wildlife, taking furbearers of any kind, or pursuing any other privilege granted by this title, to hunt for, take, trap, pursue, disturb or otherwise chase any game or wildlife or to discharge, for any reason, any firearm, arrow or other deadly weapon within or through a safety zone, or to shoot at any game or wildlife while it is within the safety zone without the specific advance permission of the lawful occupant thereof.
* * *
[34 Pa. C.S. § 2505]

SECTION 2506
Prohibitions Within Burial Grounds

(a) **General rule.** It is unlawful for any person at any time to hunt, take or trap game or wildlife of any kind or to discharge any firearm or other deadly weapon into or within, or to dress out game or wildlife within, any cemetery or other burial grounds.
Penalty. A violation of this section is a summary offense of the fourth degree.
[34 Pa. C.S. § 2506]

SECTION 2507
Restrictions on Shooting

(a) **General rule.** It is unlawful for any person during the open season for the taking of any big game other than turkey to:

(1) Shoot at any mark or target other than legal game or wildlife with a firearm of any kind or a bow and arrow.
(2) Discharge at any time any firearm or release an arrow at random in the general direction of any game or wildlife not plainly visible for the purpose of routing or frightening them.
(3) Discharge at any time any firearm or release an arrow at random or in any other manner contrary to this section.

(a) Exceptions. This section shall not be construed to apply in any manner to:

(1) The discharge of any firearm for the sole purpose of signaling for aid or assistance while in distress.

(2) The use of rifle, pistol or archery ranges owned, leased or maintained by a State or Federal military or police organization or by any regularly organized rifle, pistol, shotgun or archery range, shooting association or club while shooting at a regularly established and properly safeguarded range or to any public shooting exhibition properly safeguarded and conducted under the direction of any organization for the promotion of marksmanship.

(3) The discharge of a muzzle-loading firearm at a proper target for the purpose of safe transportation of the muzzle-loaded firearm.

(4) Shooting at a properly constructed target or mark or a dead tree protected by a natural or artificial barrier so that the ball, bullet or arrow cannot travel more than 15 yards beyond the target aimed at, after making due allowance for deflection in any direction not to exceed an angle of 45 degrees. Target shooting shall only be lawful when it is done:

(i) Upon property owned by the shooter or by a guest of the property owner.

(ii) Within 200 yards of the camp or other headquarters where the person shooting is quartered or is an invited guest or visitor.

(c) Penalty. A violation of this section is a summary offense of the fourth degree.
[34 Pa. C.S. § 2507]

──────────── **SECTION 2508** ────────────
Protection of Institutions, Parks and Resorts

(a) General rule. Subject to the posting requirements of subsection (b), it is unlawful for any person to hunt for or take any game or wildlife or to discharge a firearm or bow of any description into or upon any of the following areas:

(1) The lands, waters or premises of any public or private hospital or sanatorium or health care facility.

(2) The lands, waters or premises of any park or resort set aside for the use of the public where people may congregate in the open for health, recreation or pleasure.

(3) The lands, waters or premises of any publicly owned institution where people are hospitalized, quartered or incarcerated at public expense.

* * *

125

(c) Exceptions. Subsection (a) shall not apply to:

Any properly constructed and designated pistol, rifle, shotgun or archery range upon the lands of a hospital, sanatorium, park, resort or other institution.

* * *

[34 Pa. C.S. § 2508]

SECTION 2521
Accident Reports

(a) General rule. Every person who causes or is involved in an accident in which a human being is injured by any firearm or bow and arrow while hunting or taking game, wildlife or furbearers or incurs a self-inflicted injury with any firearm or bow and arrow while hunting or taking game, wildlife or furbearers shall render a report to the commission at Harrisburg or deliver the report to any officer of the commission on duplicate forms provided for that purpose. The report shall be delivered within 72 hours after the injury. Each 24-hour period thereafter shall constitute a separate offense. If the person is physically incapable of making the required report, it shall be the duty of the person or persons involved in the accident to designate an agent to file the report within the specified time.

(b) Penalty.

(1) A violation of this section involving a nonfatal accident is a summary offense of the fifth degree.

(2) A violation of this section involving a fatal accident is a summary offense of the fourth degree

[34 Pa. C.S. § 2521]

SECTION 2522
Shooting At or Causing Injury to Human Beings

(a) General rule. It is unlawful for any person while hunting or furtaking, through carelessness or negligence, to shoot at, injure or kill any human being through the use of a firearm, bow and arrow or other deadly weapon.

* * *

[34 Pa. C.S. § 2522]

SECTION 2523
Rendering Assistance After Accidents

(b) General rule. It is unlawful for any person who has inflicted injury or witnessed the infliction of injury to a human being with any firearm or bow and arrow, while hunting or furtaking, to flee or to fail or refuse to render immediate and full assistance to the person injured.

* * *

[34 Pa. C.S. § 2523]

SECTION 2524
Protective Material Required

(a) General rule. Unless further restricted by regulations of the commission, every person hunting for or assisting to hunt for deer, bear or woodchucks shall wear either a minimum of 250 square inches of daylight fluorescent orange-colored material on the back and front combined or, in lieu thereof, a hat of the same color material. The material shall be worn so it is visible in a 360-degree arc. Unless otherwise specified by regulations of the commission, the provision of this section shall not apply to any season for using muzzle-loading firearms only or season for using bows and arrows only.

(b) Penalty. A violation of this section is a summary offense of the fifth degree.
[34 Pa. C.S. § 2524]

SECTION 2711
Unlawful Acts Concerning Licenses

(a) General rule. Except as otherwise provided in this title, it is unlawful for any person to:

* * *

(8) Use firearms of any kind or a bow and arrow for the purpose of hunting any game or wildlife or attempting to take or kill any game or wildlife by hunting or trapping if under 12 years of age or when hunting or trapping any game or wildlife or attempting to hunt or trap any game or wildlife if between 12 and 14 years of age, unless accompanied by a parent or a person 18 years of age or older serving in loco parentis or as guardian or some other family member 18 years of age or older or when hunting if between 14 and 16 years of age, unless accompanied by a person 18 years of age or older. For the purpose of this paragraph "accompany" means close enough that verbal instructions and guidance can be easily understood. The provisions of this paragraph shall not apply to section 2363 (relating to trapping exceptions for certain persons).

* * *

[34 Pa. C.S. § 2711]

SECTION 2382
Training Dogs on Small Game

* * *

(a) Restrictions.

(1) Any dog being trained pursuant to subsection (a) shall be accompanied by and under the control of the owner or a handler.

(2) The owner or handler or any other person shall not carry a bow and arrow or a firearm fired from the shoulder while training a dog.

(3) No dog shall be permitted to kill or inflict any injury upon the pursued game or wildlife.

* * *

[34 Pa. C.S. § 2382]

SECTION 2945
---

* * *

Fox Chasing

(a) Unlawful acts. It is unlawful to:

* * *

(2) Kill or attempt to kill any fox being chased by hounds under authority of a fox chasing permit with any gun or device other than the dogs legally being used in the chase.

* * *

[34 Pa. C.S. § 2945]

MUNICIPAL REGULATION OF FIREARMS

SECTION 6120

Limitation on Municipal Regulation of Firearms & Ammunition

(a) General rule. No county, municipality or township may in any manner regulate the lawful ownership, possession, transfer or transportation of firearms, ammunition or ammunition components when carried or transported for purposes not prohibited by the laws of this Commonwealth.

(b) Definition. For the purposes of this section, the term "firearms" has the meaning given in section 5515 (relating to prohibiting of paramilitary training) but shall not include "air rifles" as defined in section 6304 (relating to sale and use of air rifles.)

[18 Pa. C.S. § 6120]

SECTION 302

(Home Rule Charters)

* * *

(e) No municipality shall enact any ordinance or take any other action dealing with the regulation of the transfer, ownership, transportation or possession of firearms.

* * *

[1972, P.L. 184, No. 62, § 302]

SECTION 3

(Powers of Second Class Cities)

Every city of the second class, in its corporate capacity, is authorized and empowered to enact ordinances for the following purposes, in addition to the other powers granted by this act:

* * *

XXVI. To prevent and restrain riots, routs, noises, disturbances or disorderly assemblies, in any street, house or place in the city; to regulate, preent and punish the discharge of fire-arms, rockets, powder, fireworks, or any other dangerous, combustible material, in the streets lots, grounds, alleys, or in the vicinity of any buildings; to prevent and punish the carrying of concealed deadly weapons; to arrest, fine, or set at work on the streets or elsewhere, all vagrants found in said city; to prevent and punish horse-racing, fast driving or riding in the streets, highways, alleys, bridges, or places in the city, and all games, practices or amusements therein likely to result in danger or damage to any person or property; and to prevent and punish the riding or driving of horses, mules, oxen, cattle, or other teams, or the passage of any vehicles drawn thereby, over, upon or across sidewalks, and to regulate the passing of the same through the public streets.

* * *

[1901, P.L. 20, No. 14, Art. 19, § 3]

SECTION 1
(Regulations by Cities)

Be it enacted, &c., That the cities of this Commonwealth be, and they are hereby, authorized to regulate or to prohibit and prevent the sale and use of fireworks, firecrackers, sparklers, and other pyrotechnics in such cities, and the unnecessary firing and discharge of firearms in or into the highways and other public places thereof, and to pass all necessary ordinances regulating or forbidding the same and prescribing penalties for their violation.

[1921, P.L. 430, No. 204, § 1]

SECTION 2403
Specific Powers (of Third Class Cities)

In addition to other powers granted by this act, the council of each city shall have power, by ordinance:

* * *

26. Regulate Guns, Et Cetera. To regulate, prohibit, and prevent the discharge of guns, rockets, powder, or any other dangerous instrument or combustible material within the city, and to prevent the carrying of concealed deadly weapons.

* * *

[1931, P.L. 932, No. 317, § 2403]

SECTION 1
General Immunity For Noise

All owners of rifle, pistol, silhouette, skeet, trap, blackpowder or other ranges in this Commonwealth shall be exempt and immune from any civil action or criminal prosecution in any matter relating to noise or noise pollution resulting from the normal and accepted shooting activity on ranges, provided that the owners of the ranges are in compliance with any

applicable noise control laws or ordinances extant at the time construction of the range was initiated.
[1988, P.L. 452, No. 74, § 1]

LETHAL WEAPONS TRAINING ACT

———————— SECTION 1 ————————
Short Title

This act shall be known and may be cited as the "Lethal Weapons Training Act."
[1974, P.L. 705, No. 235, § 1]

———————— SECTION 2 ————————
Legislative Findings and Purpose

(a) The General Assembly finds that there are private detectives, investigators, watchmen, security guards and patrolmen, privately employed within this Commonwealth who carry and use lethal weapons including firearms as an incidence of their employment and that there have been various tragic incidents involving these individuals which occurred because of unfamiliarity with the handling of weapons. The General Assembly also finds that there is presently no training required for such privately employed agents in the handling of lethal weapons or in the knowledge of law enforcement and the protection of rights of citizens, and that such training would be beneficial to the safety of the citizens of this Commonwealth.

(b) It is the purpose of this act to provide for the education, training and certification of such privately employed agents who, as an incidence to their employment, carry lethal weapons through a program administered or approved by the Commissioner of the Pennsylvania State Police.
[1974, P.L. 705, No. 235, § 2]

———————— SECTION 3 ————————

Definitions. As used in this act:

"Commissioner" means the Commissioner of the Pennsylvania State Police.

"Full-time police officer" means any employee of a city, borough, town, township or county police department assigned to law enforcement duties who works a minimum of two hundred days per year. The term does not include persons employed to check parking meters or to perform only administrative duties, nor does it include auxiliary and fire police.

"Lethal weapons" include but are not limited to firearms and other weapons calculated to produce death or serious bodily harm. A concealed billy club is a lethal weapon. The chemical mace or any similar substance shall not be considered as "lethal weapons" for the purposes of this act.

"Privately employed agents" include any person employed for the purpose of providing watch guard, protective patrol, detective or criminal investigative services either for another for a fee or for his employer. Privately employed agents do not include local, State or Federal Government employees or those police officers commissioned by the Governor under the act of February 27, 1865 (P.L. 225, No. 228). The term shall include a police officer of a municipal authority.

"Program" means the education and training program established and administered or approved by the commissioner in accordance with this act.

[1974, P.L. 705, No. 235, § 3]

SECTION 4
Education and Training Program

(a) An education and training program in the handling of lethal weapons, law enforcement and protection of rights of citizens shall be established and administered or approved by the commissioner in accordance with the provisions of this act.

(b) All privately employed agents, except those who have been granted a waiver from compliance herewith by the commissioner who, as an incidence to their employment, carry a lethal weapon shall be required to attend the program established by subsection (a) of this section in accordance with the requirements or regulations established by the commissioner and, upon satisfactory completion of such program, shall be entitled to certification by the commissioner.

(c) Except for colleges and universities, no nongovernment employer of a privately employed agent who, as an incidence to his employment, carries a lethal weapon, shall own, operate, or otherwise participate in, directly or indirectly, the establishment or administration of the program established by subsection (a) of this section.

[1974, P.L. 705, No. 235, § 4]

SECTION 5
Power and Duties of Commissioner

The commissioner shall have the power and duty:

(1) To implement and administer or approve the minimum courses of study and training for the program in the handling of lethal weapons, law enforcement and protection of the rights of citizens.

(2) To implement and administer or approve physical and psychological testing and screening of the candidate for the purpose of barring from the program those not physically or mentally fit to handle lethal weapons. However, candidates who are full-time police officers and have successfully completed a physical and psychological examination as a prerequisite to employment or to continued employment by their local police departments or who have been continuously employed as full-time police officers since June 18, 1974 shall not be required to undergo any physical or psychological testing and screening procedures so implemented.

(3) To issue certificates of approval to schools approved by the commissioner and to withdraw certificates of approval from those schools disapproved by the commissioner.

(4) To certify instructors pursuant to the minimum qualifications established by the commissioner.

(5) To consult and cooperate with universities, colleges, community colleges and institutes for the development of specialized courses in handling lethal weapons, law enforcement and protection of the rights of citizens.

(6) To consult and cooperate with departments and agencies of this Commonwealth and other states and the Federal Government concerned with similar training.

(7) To certify those individuals who have satisfactorily completed basic educational and training requirements as established by the commissioner and to issue appropriate certificates to such persons.

(8) To visit and inspect approved schools at least one a year.

(9) In the event that the commissioner implements and administers a program, to collect reasonable charges from the students enrolled therein to pay for the costs of the program.

(10) To make such rules and regulations and to perform such other duties as may be reasonably necessary or appropriate to implement the education and training program.

(11) To grant waivers from compliance with the provisions of this act applicable to privately employed agents who have completed a course of instruction in a training program approved by the commissioner. *[1974, P.L. 705, No. 235, § 5]*

SECTION 6
Certificate of Qualification

(a) Any person desiring to enroll in such program shall make application to the commissioner, on a form to be prescribed by the commissioner.

(b) The application shall be signed and verified by the applicant. It shall include his full name, age, residence, present and previous occupations and such other information that may be required by the commissioner to show the good character, competency and integrity of the applicant.

(c) The application shall be personally presented by the applicant at an office of the Pennsylvania State Police where his fingerprints shall be affixed thereto. The application shall be accompanied by two current photographs of the applicant of a size and nature to be prescribed by the commissioner and a thirty-five dollar ($35) application fee, unless the applicant is a full-time police officer, in which case no application fee shall be required. Thereafter the application shall be forwarded to the commissioner.

(d) The fingerprints of the applicant shall be examined by the Pennsylvania State Police and the Federal Bureau of Investigation to determine if he has been convicted of or has pleaded guilty or nolo contendere to a crime of violence. The commissioner shall have the power to waive the requirement of Federal Bureau of Investigation examination. Any fee charged by the Federal agency shall be paid by the applicant.

(e) No application shall be accepted if the applicant is under the age of eighteen.

(f) After the application has been processed and if the commissioner determines that the applicant is eighteen years of age and has not been convicted of or has not pleaded guilty or nolo contendere to a crime of violence, and has satisfied any other requirements prescribed by him under his powers and duties pursuant to section 5, he shall issue a certificate of qualification which shall entitle the applicant to enroll in an approved program.

[1974, P.L. 705, No. 235, § 6]

SECTION 7
Certification and Fee

(a) A certification fee of not more than fifteen dollars ($15) shall be paid by each individual satisfactorily completing the program prior to the receipt of a certificate.

(b) The commissioner shall furnish to each individual satisfactorily completing the program, an appropriate wallet or billfold size copy of the certificate, which shall include a photograph of the individual thereon.

(c) Every certified individual shall carry his wallet or billfold size certificate on his person as identification during the time when he is on duty or going to and from duty and carrying a lethal weapon.

(d) Certification whall be for a period five years.

(e) Privately employed agents who, as an incidence to their employment, carry a lethal weapon shall be required to renew their certification within six months prior to the expiration of their certificate. The commissioner shall prescribe the manner in which the certification shall be renewed, and may charge a nominal renewal fee therefore, not to exceed fifteen dollars ($15).

[1974, P.L. 705, No. 235, § 7]

SECTION 8
Good Standing

(a) Privately employed agents must possess a valid certificate whenever on duty or going to and from duty and carrying a lethal weapon

(b) Whenever an employer of a privately employed agent subject to the provisions of this act discharges him for cause, the employer shall notify the commissioner of such within five days of the discharge.

(c) The commissioner may revoke and invalidate any certificate issued to a privately employed agent under this act whenever he learns that false,

133

fraudulent or misstated information appears on the original or renewal application or whenever he learns of a change of circumstances that would render an employee ineligible for original certification.
[1974, P.L. 705, No. 235, §8]

SECTION 9
Penalties

(a) Any privately employed agent who in the course of his employ carries a lethal weapon, and who fails to comply with subsection (b) of section 4 or with subsection (a) of section 8 of this act, shall be guilty of a misdemeanor and upon conviction shall be subject to imprisonment of not more than one year or payment of a fine not exceeding one thousand dollars ($1,000), or both.

(b) Any privately employed agent who in the course of his employ carries a lethal weapon, and who violates subsection (c) of section 7 of this act shall be guilty of a summary offense, and, upon concviction, shall pay a fine not exceeding fifty dollars ($50).
[1974, P.L. 705, No. 235, § 9]

SECTION 10
Prohibited Act

(a) No individual certified under this act shall carry an inoperative or model firearm while employed and he shall carry only a powder actuated firearm approved by the commissioner.
[1974, P.L. 705, No. 235 § 10]

SECTION 10.1
Active Police Officers

All active police officers subject to the training provisions of the act of June 18, 1974 (P.L. 359, No. 120), referred to as the Municipal Police Education and Training Law, shall be granted a waiver of the training requirements of this act upon presentation to the commissioner of evidence of their completion of the training requirements of the Municipal Police Education and Training Law and the successful completion of a biennial firearms qualification examination administered by their respective police agency.
[1974, P.L. 705, No. 235 § 10.1]

OTHER TRAINING AND EDUCATION

SECTION 9

Police Training Mandatory; Penalties

All political subdivisions of the Commonwealth or groups of political subdivisions acting in concert shall be required to train all members of their police departments prior to actually enforcing criminal laws, enforcing moving traffic violations under 75 Pa. C.S. (relating to vehicles) or being

134

authorized to carry a firearm after the effective date of this act, pursuant to the provisions of this act.

(b) Those municipal police officers employed on the effective date of this subsection shall be able to perform criminal or traffic duties and be authorized to carry a firearm until certified by the commission, but no longer than one year from their date of employment.

* * *

[1974, P.L. 359, No. 120, § 9]

SECTION 1.8

No constable or deputy constable shall carry or use a firearm in the performance of his or her duties unless he or she is currently certified or qualified in firearms pursuant to at least one of the following:

(a) The act of June 18, 1974 (P.L. 359, No. 120), referred to as the Municipal Police Education and Training Law.

(b) The act of October 10, 1974 (P.L. 705, No. 235), known as the Lethal Weapons Training Act.

(c) The act of February 9, 1984 (P.L. 3, No. 2), known as the Deputy Sheriffs' Education and Training Act.

(d) Any other firearms program which has been approved by the board with the review and approval of the commission.
[1917, P.L. 1158, No. 401, § 1.8]

DOMESTIC RELATIONS

SECTION 6102
Definitions

(a) General rule. The following words and phrases when used in this chapter shall have the meanings given to them in this section unless the context clearly indicates otherwise:

"Abuse." The occurrence of one or more of the following acts between family or household members, sexual or intimate partners or persons who share biological parenthood:

(1) Attempting to cause or intentionally, knowingly or recklessly causing bodily injury, serious bodily injury, rape, spousal sexual assault or involuntary deviate sexual intercourse with or without a deadly weapon.

* * *

[23 Pa. C.S. § 6102]

SECTION 6108
Relief

(a) General rule. the court may grant any protection order or approve any consent agreement to bring about a cessation of abuse of the plaintiff or minor children. The order or agreement may include:

* * *

Ordering the defendant to temporarily relinquish to the sheriff the defendant's weapons which have been used or been threatened to be used in an incident of abuse against the plaintiff or the minor children. The court's order shall provide for the return of the weapons to the defendant subject to any restrictions and conditions as the court shall deem appropriate to protect the plaintiff or minor children from further abuse through the use of weapons.

* * *

[23 Pa. C.S. § 6108]

SECTION 6113
Arrest for Violation of Order

* * *

(a) Seizure of weapons. Subsequent to an arrest, the police officer shall seize all weapons used or threatened to be used during the violation of the protection order or during prior incidents of abuse. As soon as it is reasonably possible, the arresting officer shall deliver the confiscated weapons to the office of the sheriff. The sheriff shall maintain possession of the weapons until the court issues an order specifying the weapons to be relinquished and the persons to whom the weapons shall be relinquished.

* * *

[23 Pa. C.S. § 6113]

SECTION 2711
Probable Cause Arrests in Domestic Violence Cases

* * *

(b) Seizure of weapons. The arresting police officer shall seize all weapons used by the defendant in the commission of the alleged offense.

* * *

[18 Pa. C.S. § 2711]

CRIMES AND OFFENSES GENERALLY
SECTION 508
Use of Force in Law Enforcement

(a) Peace officer's use of force in making arrest.

    (1) A peace officer, or any person whom he has summoned or directed to assist him, need not retreat or desist from efforts to make a lawful arrest because of resistance or threatened resistance to the arrest. He is justified in the use of any force which he believes to be necessary to effect the arrest and of any force which he believes to be necessary to defend himself or another from bodily harm while making the arrest. However, he is justified in using deadly force only when he believes that such force is necessary to prevent death or serious bodily injury to himself or such other person, or when he believes both that:

(i) such force is necessary to prevent the arrest from being defeated by resistance or escape; and

(ii) the person to be arrested has committed or attempted a forcible felony or is attempting to escape and possesses a deadly weapon, or otherwise indicates that he will endanger human life or inflict serious bodily injury unless arrested without delay.

* * *

[18 Pa. C.S. § 508]

───────────────── **SECTION 22** ─────────────────

Riotous Assemblies; Proclamation To Disperse; Penalty For Failure To Disperse; Possession of Firearms or Deadly Weapons

If any persons shall be unlawfully, riotously and tumultuously assembled together, to the number of twelve or more, so as to endanger the public peace of said police district, it shall be the duty of said marshal (the marshal of police) in person, or in case of his absence or inability ot command, of the officer then in command of said police, to go among the said rioters, or as near to them as he can safely to, and then and there with a loud voice make proclamation in the name of the Commonwealth, requiring and commanding all persons there so unlawfully, riotously or tumultuously assembled, and all other persons not being there on duty as police, immediately to disperse themselves and peaceably to depart to their habitations, or to their lawful business; and if such persons, notwithstanding such proclamation made, unlawfully, riotously or tumultuously remain or continue together, to the number of twelve or more after such proclamation made, then such continuing together shall be adjudged a misdemeanor, and the said offenders upon conviction thereof shall be sentenced to undergo a solitary confinement at labor in the county prison, for a period of not less than one month nor more than two years, and any person arrested upon whose person, or in whose possession shall be found firearms, or any othe deaedly weapon, shall be deemed guilty of an intention to riot, whether said fire-arms or deadly weapon shall be used or not, unless the contrary can be satisfactorily established, and punished accordingly.

[1850, P.L. 666, No. 390 § 22]

SECTION 5501
Riot

A person is guilty of riot, a felony of the third degree, if he participates with two or more others in a course of disorderly conduct:

(1) with intent to commit or facilitate the commission of a felony or misdemeanor;

(2) with intent to prevent or coerce official action; or

(3) when the actor or any other participant to the knowledge of the actor uses or plans to use a firearm or other deadly weapon.

[18 Pa. C.S. § 5501]

SECTION 5515
Prohibiting of Paramilitary Training

(a) Definitions. As used in this section the following words and phrases shall have the meanings given to them in this subsection:

"Firearm." Any weapon which is designed to or may readily be converted to expel any projectile by the action of an explosive; or the frame or receiver of any such weapon.

"Law enforcement officer." Any officer or employee of the United States, any state, any political subdivision of a state or the District of Columbia and such term shall specifically include, but shall not be limited to, members of the National Guard, as defined in 10 U.S.C. § 101 (9), members of the organized militia of any state or territory of the United States, the commonwealth of Puerto Rico or the District of Columbia, not included within the definition of National Guard as defined by 10 U.S.C. § 101 (9) and members of the armed forces of the United States.

(b) Prohibited training.

(1) Whoever teaches or demonstrates to any other person the use, application or making of any firearm, explosive or incendiary device or technique capable of causing injury or death to persons, knowing or having reason to know or intending that same will be unlawfully employed for use in, or in furtherance of, a civil disorder commits a misdemeanor of the first degree.

(2) Whoever assembles with one or more persons for the purpose of training with, practicing with or being instructed in the use of any firearm, explosive or incendiary device or technique capable of causing injury or death to persons, said person intending to employ unlawfully the same for use in or in furtherance of a civil disorder commits a misdemeanor of the first degree.

(c) **Exemptions.** Nothing contained in this section shall make unlawful any act of any law enforcement officer which is performed in the lawful performance of his official duties.

(d) **Excluded activities.** Nothing contained in this section shall make unlawful any activity of the Game Commission, Fish and Boat Commission, or any law enforcement agency, or any hunting club, rifle club, rifle range, pistol range, shooting range or other program or individual instruction intended to teach the safe handling or use of firearms, archery equipment or other weapons or techniques employed in connection with lawful sports or other lawful activities.
[18 Pa. C.S. § 5515]

SECTION 907
Possessing Instruments of Crime

(a) **Criminal instruments generally.** A person commits a misdemeanor of the first degree if he possesses any instrument of crime with intent to employ it criminally.

(b) **Possession of weapon.** A person commits a misdemeanor of the first degree if he possesses a firearm or other weapon concealed upon his person with intent to employ it criminally.

(c) **Definitions.** As used in this section the following words and phrases shall have the meanings given to them in this subsection:

"Instrument of crime."

(1) Anything specially made or specially adapted for criminal use; or
(2) anything commonly used for criminal purposes and possessed by the actor under circumstances not manifestly appropriate for lawful uses it may have.

"Weapon." Anything readily capable of lethal use and possessed under circumstances not manifestly appropriate for lawful uses which it may have. The term includes a firearm which is not loaded or lacks a clip or other component to render it immediately operable, and components which can readily be assembled into a weapon.
[18 Pa. C.S. § 907]

SECTION 908
Prohibited Offensive Weapons

(a) **Offense defined.** A person commits a misdemeanor of the first degree if, except as authorized by law, he makes repairs, sells, or otherwise deals in, uses, or possesses any offensive weapon.

(b) Exceptions.

(1) It is a defense under this section for the defendant to prove by a preponderance of evidence that he possessed or dealt with the weapon solely as a curio or in a dramatic performance, or that, with the exception of a bomb, grenade or incendiary device, he complied with the National Firearms Act (26 U.S.C. § 5801 et seq.), or that he possessed it briefly in consequence of having found it or taken it from an aggressor, or under circumstances similarly negativing any intent or likelihood that the weapon would be used unlawfully.

(2) This section does not apply to police forensic firearms experts or police forensic firearms laboratories. Also exempt from this section are forensic firearms experts or forensic firearms laboratories operating in the ordinary course of business and engaged in lawful operation who notify in writing, on an annual basis, the chief or head of any police force or police department of a city, and, elsewhere, the sheriff of a county in which they are located, of the possession, type and use of offensive weapons.

(3) This section shall not apply to any person who makes, repairs, sells or otherwise deals in, uses or possesses any firearm for purposes not prohibited by the laws of this Commonwealth.

(c) Definition. As used in this section, the following words and phrases shall have the meanings given to them in this subsection:

"Firearm." Any weapon which is designed to or may readily be converted to expel any projectile by the action of an explosive, or the frame or receiver of any such weapon.

"Offensive weapons." Any bomb, grenade, machine gun, sawed off shotgun with a barel less than 18 inches, firearm specially made or specially adapted for concealment or silent discharge, any blackjack, sandbag, metal knuckles, dagger, knife, razor or cutting instrument, the blade of which is exposed in an automatic way by switch, push-button, spring mechanism, or otherwise, or other implement for the infliction of serious bodily injury which serves no common lawful purpose.

* * *

[18 Pa. C.S. § 908]

———————————— **SECTION 2301** ————————————
Definitions

Subject to additional definitions contained in subsequent provisions of this article which are applicable to specific chapters or other provisions of this article, the following words and phrases, when used in this article shall have, unless the context clearly indicates otherwise, the meanings given to them in this section:

"Deadly weapon." Any firearm, whether loaded or unloaded, or any device designed as a weapon and capable of producing death or serious bodily injury, or any other device or instrumentality which, in the manner in which it is used or intended to be used, is calculated or likely to produce death or serious bodily injury.

[18 Pa. C.S. § 2301]

SECTION 5106
Failure To Report Injuries By Firearm or Criminal Act

(a) Offense defined. A physician, intern or resident, or any person conducting, managing or in charge of any hospital or pharmacy, or in charge of any ward or part of a hospital, to who shall come or be brought any person:

(1) suffering from any wound or other injury inflicted by his own act or by the act of another by means of a deadly weapon as defined in section 2301 of this title (relating to definitions); or

(2) upon whom injuries have been inflicted in violation of any penal law of this Commonwealth; commits a summary offense if he fails to report such injuries immediately, both by telephone and in writing, to the chief of police or other head of the police department of the local government, or to the Pennsylvania State Police. The report shall state the name of the injured person, if known, his whereabouts and the character and extent of his injuries.

* * *

[18 Pa. C.S. § 5106]

SECTION 5105
Hindering Apprehension or Prosecution

(a) Offense defined. A person commits an offense if, with intent to hinder the apprehension, prosecution, conviction or punishment of another for crime, he:

* * *

(2) provides or aids in providing a weapon, transportation, disguise or other means of avoiding apprehension or effecting escape;

* * *

[18 Pa. C.S. § 5105]

SECTION 2701
Simple Assault

(a) Offense defined. A person is guilty of assault if he:

* * *

(2) negligently causes bodily injury to another with a deadly weapon; or

   * * *

[18 Pa. C.S. § 2701]

SECTION 2702
Aggravated Assault

(a) Offense defined. A person is guilty of aggravated assault if he:

   * * *

   (4) attempts to cause or intentionally or knowingly causes bodily injury to another with a deadly weapon; or

   * * *

[18 Pa. C.S. § 2702]

SECTION 5122
Weapons or Implements for Escape

(a) Offenses defined.

   (1) A person commits a misdemeanor of the first degree if he unlawfully introduces within a detention facility; correctional institution or mental hospital, or unlawfully provides an inmate thereof with any weapon, tool, implement, or other thing which may be used for escape.

   (2) An inmate commits a misdemeanor of the first degree if he unlawfully procures, makes or otherwise provides himself with, or unlawfully has in his possession or under his control, any weapon.

   * * *

(b) Definitions.

   * * *

   (2) As used in this section the word "weapon" means any implement readily capable of lethal use and shall include any firearm, knife, dagger, razor, other cutting or stabbing implement or club, including any item which has been modified or adapted so that it can be used as a firearm, knife, dagger, razor, other cutting or stabbing implement, or club. The word "firearm" includes an unloaded firearm and the unassembled components of a firearm.

[18 Pa. C.S. § 5122]

SECTION 6801
Loss of Property Rights To Commonwealth

(a) Forfeitures generally. The following shall be subject to forfeiture to the Commonwealth and no property right shall exist in them:

   (7) Any firearms, including, but not limited to, rifles, shotguns, pistols, revolvers, machine guns, zip guns or any type of prohibited offensive weapon, as that term is defined in 18 Pa. C.S. (relating to crimes and offenses), which are used or intended for use to facilitate a violation of The Controlled Substance, Drug, Device and Cosmetic Act. Such operable firearms as are found in close proximity to illegally possessed controlled substances shall be rebuttably presumed to be used or intended for use to facilitate a violation of The Controlled Substance, Drug, Device and Cosmetic Act. All weapons forfeited under this section shall be immediately destroyed by the receiving law enforcement agency.

* * *

[42 Pa. C.S. § 6801]

SENTENCING
SECTION 106
Classes of Offenses

(a) General Rule. An offense defined by this title for which a sentence of death or of imprisonment is authorized constitutes a crime. The classes of crime are:

(1) Murder of the first degree or of the second degree.
(2) Felony of the first degree.
(3) Felony of the second degree.
(4) Felony of the third degree.
(5) Misdemeanor of the first degree.
(6) Misdemeanor of the second degree.
(7) Misdemeanor of the third degree.

(b) Classification of crimes

(1) A crime is a murder of the first degree or of the second degree if it is so designated in this title or if a person convicted of criminal homicide may be sentenced in accordance with the provisions of section 1102 of this title (relating to sentence for murder of the first degree or of the second degree).
(2) A crime is a felony of the first degree if it is so designated in this title or if a person convicted thereof may be sentenced to a term of imprisonment, the maximum of which is more than ten years.
(3) A crime is a felony of the second degree if it is so designated in this title or if a person convicted thereof may be sentenced to a term of imprisonment, the maximum of which is not more than ten years.
(4) A crime is a felony of the third degree if it is so designated in this title or if a person convicted thereof may be sentenced to a term of imprisonment, the maximum of which is not more than seven years.

(5) A crime declared to be a felony, without specification of degree, is of the third degree.

(6) A crime is a misdemeanor of the first degree if it is so designated in this title or if a person convicted thereof may be sentenced to a term of imprisonment, the maximum of which is not more than five years.

(7) A crime is a misdemeanor of the second degree if it is so designated in this title or if a person conviceted thereof may be sentenced to a term of imprisonment, the maximum of which is not more than two years.

(8) A crime is a misdemeanor of the third degree if it is so designated in this title or if a person convicted thereof may be sentenced to a term of imprisonment, the maximum of which is not more than one year.

(9) A crime declared to be a misdemeanor, without specification of degree, is of the third degree.

(c) **Summary offenses.** An offense defined by this title constitutes a summary offense if:

(1) it is so designated in this title, or in a statute other than this title; or

(2) if a person convicted thereof may be sentenced to a term of imprisonment, the maximum of which is not more than 90 days.

(d) **Other crimes.** Any offense declared by law to constitute a crime, without specification of the class thereof, is a misdemeanor of the second degree, if the maximum sentence does not make it a felony under this section.

(e) **Section applicable to other statutes.** An offense hereafter defined by any statute other than this title shall be classified as provided in this section. *[18 Pa. C.S. § 106]*

SECTION 9712
Sentences For Offenses Committed With Firearms

(a) **Mandatory sentence.** Any person who is convicted in any court of this Commonwealth of murder of the third degree, voluntary manslaughter, rape, involuntary deviate sexual intercourse, robbery as defined in 18 Pa. C.S. § 3701 (a) (1) (i), (ii) or (iii) (relating to robbery), aggravated assault as defined in 18 Pa. C.S. § 2702 (a) (1) (relating to aggravated assault) or kidnapping, or who is convicted of attempt to commit any of these crimes, shall, if the person visibly possessed a firearm or a replica of a firearm, whether or not the firearm or replica was loaded or functional, that placed the victim in reasonable fear of death or serious bodily injury, during the commission of the offense, be sentenced to a minimum sentence of at least five years of total confinement notwithstanding any other provision of this title or other statute to the contrary. Such persons shall not be eligible for parole, probation, work release or furlough.

* * *

(b) **Definitions.** As used in this section, the following words and phrases shall have the meanings given to them in this subsection:

"Firearm." Any weapon, including a starter gun, which will or is designed to or may readily be converted to expel a projectile by the action of an explosive or the expansion of gas therin.

"Replica of a firearm." An item that can reasonably be perceived to be a firearm.

[42 Pa. C.S. § 9712; Act 17]

SECTION 9754
Order Of Probation

* * *

(c) **Specific conditions.** The court may as a condition of its order require the defendant:

    (7) To have in his possession no firearm or other dangerous weapon unless granted written permission.

    * * *

[42 Pa. C.S. § 9754]

SECTION 9763
Sentence Of Intermediate Punishment

* * *

(b) **Conditions generally.** The court may attach any of the following conditions upon the defendant as it deems necessary:

    * * *

    (9) To not possess a firearm or other dangerous weapon unless granted written permission.

    * * *

[42 Pa. C.S. § 9763]

PART III
PENNSYLVANIA STATUTE INDEX

Use this index to find the page in the book, on which any statute (law) mentioned in the text can be found.

TITLE (Pa. C.S.)	SECTION	PAGE
34	2308	120
34	2310	120
34	2311	121
34	2322	122
34	2325	122
34	2363	122
34	2382	127
34	2501	123
34	2503	123
34	2505	124
34	2506	124
34	2507	124
34	2508	125
34	2521	126
34	2522	126
34	2523	126
34	2524	127
34	2704	122
34	2711	127
34	2945	128
35	7301	110
42	6308	110
42	6801	143
42	9712	144
42	9754	145
42	9763	145
75	7727	124

SESSION	P.L.	ACT	SECTION	PAGE
1850	666	390	22	137
1917	1158	401	1 .8	135
1901	20	14	Art. 19, § 3	128
1921	430	204	1	129
1929	177	175	712	118
1931	932	317	2403	129
1972	184	62	302	128
1974	359	120	9	134
1974	705	235	1	130
1974	705	235	2	130
1974	705	235	3	130
1974	705	235	4	131
1974	705	235	5	131
1974	705	235	6	132
1974	705	235	7	133
1974	705	235	8	133
1974	705	235	9	134
1974	705	235	10	134
1974	705	235	10 .1	134
1988	452	74	1	129

GUN OWNERS:
NEED ANOTHER COPY OF THIS BOOK?

Please purchase additional copies from your local retailer or gun club.

If you cannot find this book in your area, you may order additional copies direct from the publisher. *Please use the order form supplied at the back of this book.*

SPORTSMEN'S CLUBS, RETAILERS & BOOKSTORES
SELL THIS BOOK!

This book is available for resale, for fundraising and for premium use *(give a copy free to customers who make a qualifying purchase).* Small minimum order. Displays depicted below are provided *free* with orders.

For information call:
800-542-9001
412-279-5012 FAX
412-279-0672 Alleg. Cty.

FLOOR DISPLAY

COUNTERTOP DISPLAY

PENNSYLVANIA GUN LAW UPDATE

We have assembled a special *two-part* package for readers of this book at a *very special price.*

PART A
(To be mailed to you immediately upon receipt of your order.)

- Learn how to get a copy of the *Pennsylvania Sportsmen's News* - with information on who, in our state and federal government is on the side of gun owners, and who is not. You *can't always tell* by what the legislators say . . . because many of them tell two completely different stories! Get the truth from the *Pennsylvania Sportsmen's News.*

- FIJA, the Fully Informed Jury Association, informs Americans that jurors have the right to judge not only the guilt or innocence of defendants, but also the law itself; and can find a defendant not guilty, even if directed otherwise by the trial judge. Someday you may be the juror . . . or the defendant. Learn how to get a free juror kit from FIJA.

- Here are six items, of which three could save your life . . . or the life of a friend or family member. The other three can save you money . . . a few dollars . . . or even a few hundred dollars a year. You may have seen some of these in retail stores, where their total cost would be $8.50. All are included in Part A.

Imagine that one day you open your checking account statement, thinking you had, say $1250 in it, and discover instead that your balance was only $75 because a check THAT YOU DID NOT WRITE, for $1155 had cleared your account. And that you will not be able to get your money back. If you order merchandise by phone, using a credit card, as many gun owners do, you are especially vulnerable. Learn how this happens . . . and what you can do to avoid it.

PART B

(To be mailed after the legislature acts on the proposed amendments.)

The book you are reading will tell you everything that's known about how the new gun laws affect current, and would-be, gun owners, as of October 1996. But changes in these laws - to eliminate "traps" that could take away your guns . . . or your freedom - are being proposed by gun owners organizations. we will publish all the upcoming changes in the GUN LAW Update.

TOTAL PACKAGE COST: $5

. . . which includes *everything* described on these two pages. Please note that also included in the $5 is *postage* for *both* mailings, Pennsylvania *sales tax* and a *donation* to the Pennsylvania Sportsmen's League, whose *unpaid* volunteers are working to preserve your right to own and use rifles, shotguns and handguns free of unnecessary government regulations.

Please use Order Form on the next page.

CONSUMER ORDER FORM

Instead of cutting up this book, you may prefer to make a copy of this Order Form on any copying machine.

Use this Order Form to order *additional copies of this book*, and to order the *Pennsylvania Gun Law Update*. Please use *one copy* of the Order Form for *each address* to which you would like something sent.

PENNSYLVANIA GUN LAW GUIDE
(THIS BOOK)

_____ x $7.95 . . . . _____
No. of Copies

Postage + Handling + Sales Tax

First Copy . . . . ___$1.55___

Each Additional Copy @ 0.50 . . . . ._____

PENNSYLVANIA GUN LAW UPDATE
Part A + Part B

_____ x $5.00 (includes Sales Tax/Postage/Handling) . . _____
No. of Copies

TOTAL ENCLOSED [_____]

*Please enclose payment by check or money order. Sorry we **cannot** accept credit cards or C.O.D.'s. Thank you.*

> **Mail To:** ABELexpress-Publishers, 230 East Main St., Carnegie, PA 15106
> Have a question? Call 412-279-0672 (Alleg. Cty.) or 800-542-9001.

- -

THIS IS YOUR MAILING LABEL - PLEASE PRINT NEATLY

_____
Name

_____
Street Address or P.O. Box

_____
City   State   Zip

(   )
_____
Telephone - Day (In case we have a question about your order)

OTHER PUBLICATIONS BY KEN ABEL

- *The Yiddishe Kup Dictionary,* published September 1996
- *Table Tipper™* and *Tips on Tipping™,* published April 1996
- *Your Complete Guide to the Solar Eclipse of May 10, 1994,* (with B. Ralph Chou), published 1994
- *The Emergency Hotline Card,* published 1992
- *The Tongue-in-Cheek Guide to Pittsburgh,* (with Jackie Abel), published 1992
- *Your Complete Guide to the Solar Eclipse of January 4, 1992,* (with Joe Rao), published 1991
- *Tip Table/Tips on Tipping,* published 1988

FORTHCOMING BOOKS BY KEN ABEL

- *The Mini Tongue-in-Cheek Guide to Pittsburgh,* tentative publication date - November 1996
- *Healing Yourself with Bio-Magnetism: Ancient Discovery, Modern Applications,* tentative publ. date - July 1997
- *The Million Dollar Book of Business Know-How,* (with Jackie Abel), tentative publ. date - September 1997

BOOKS PUBLISHED BY ABELexpress

- *Your Easy Guide to the Care, Training and Breeding of Common Green Iguanas,* by Dolly Ellerbrock, published 1995
- *Are You a Real Pittsburgher?,* by Eric Schuman, published 1995
- *NASA Ref. Publ. 1344, July 1994,* abr. reprint, published 1993
- *NASA Ref. Publ. 1318, October 1993,* abr. reprint, published 1993
- *NASA Ref. Publ. 1178, July 1987,* abr. reprint, published 1993

FORTHCOMING BOOKS FROM ABELexpress

- *Psoriasis: Treatments That Work, The Self-Healing Handbook,* by Elliott D. Derzaph, tentative publ. date - February 1997
- *The Step-by-Step Guide to Caring For the Homebound,* by Gerrie L. Cockburn, tentative publ. date - February 1997
- *The Foot Book,* by Dr. John Lazar, tentative publ. date - Sept. 1997